ALCOHOLICS ANONYMOUS UNMASKED

Deception and Deliverance

SHARING
212 E. 7th St.
Mt. Carmel, PA 17851-2211

All Scripture quotations are from the King James Version of the Holy Bible.

Cover design and layout: Sandra Schappert

Library of Congress Catalog Card Number 91-76487

Sharing
212A E. 7th Street
Mt. Carmel, PA 17851-2211

ISBN 1-56043-449-X

For Worldwide Distribution

Printed in the U.S.A.

Table of Contents

1. AA'S CO-FOUNDERS

Some of our clergymen, court systems, hospitals, and other facilities recommend Alcoholics Anonymous (AA) and its program to the alcoholics and their hurting families.[1] Even though AA is a highly visible and eminently recognized organization, its history seems to be hidden from most people. Since AA has a most interesting history, it would be worthwhile to spend some time exploring its origins as well as looking at the lives of its co-founders, William Wilson and Robert Smith, M.D., known affectionately in AA circles as "Bill W." and "Dr. Bob." Both men had been considered to be "hopeless" drunks.[2]

William Griffith Wilson (November 26, 1895-January 24, 1971), the son of Emily and Gilman Barrows Wilson, was born in East Dorset, Vermont. On January 24, 1918, he married Lois Burnham. It was while he was serving in the military that Bill took to drinking. After the war, he studied law at the Brooklyn Law School, but by 1931 he had a serious drinking problem which started to interfere with his career. Although he made promise after promise to stop drinking, he was unable to do so.[3] Soon, however, he was to find some help for his problem.

In November 1934, he learned from an old friend, Ebby, how the Oxford Group was able to sometimes help alcoholics; Ebby himself was a recent example.[4]

Bill Meets Ebby

This is how Bill describes that meeting with Ebby:

...one afternoon the telephone rang. It was my old boarding-school friend and drinking companion, Ebby. Even over the phone I somehow knew that he was sober. I could not remember a time when he had been sober in New York City. Long ago I had marked him for a hopeless case. I had heard in fact that they were going to put him away because of alcoholic insanity. Eagerly I said, "Come right on over. We'll talk about the good old days." Now why did I say that? It was because my present was unbearable and I knew there was to be no future. Soon Ebby stood beaming in the doorway. Then he was sitting across the kitchen from me. There was a big crock of gin and pineapple juice between us.

Immediately I felt that there was something different about Ebby. It was not only that he was sober. I could not put a finger on what it was. I offered him a drink and he refused. Then I asked him, "What's this all about? You say you aren't drinking. But you also say you aren't on the water wagon, either. What's up?"

"Well," said Ebby, "I've got religion."

What a crusher that was—Ebby and religion! Maybe his alcoholic insanity had become religious insanity. It was an awful letdown. I had been educated at a wonderful engineering college where somehow I had gathered the impression that man was God. But I had to be polite, so I said, "What brand of religion have you got, Ebby?" "Oh," he said, "I don't think it has got any special brand name. I just fell in with a group of people, the Oxford Groups.... Now," he added, "I know you are going to gag on this, but they taught me that I should try to pray to whatever God I thought there was for the power to carry out these simple precepts. And if I did not believe there was any God, then I had better try the experiment of praying to whatever God there *might* be. And you know, Bill, it's a queer thing, but even before I had done all this, just as soon as I decided that I would try with an open mind, it seemed to me that my drinking problem was lifted right out of me. It wasn't like the water wagon business at all. This time I felt completely released of the desire, and I have not had a drink for months."

Ebby didn't try to pressure or evangelize me, and pretty soon he left. [Emphasis in the original.][5]

Bill's Last Drunk

In spite of Ebby's enthusiasm, Bill continued to drink for several more days, but then he decided to try some "religious investigation." He thought about Sam Shoemaker's Calvary Church. Sam had a mission there where Ebby's Oxford Group met. Bill went to a meeting and came home hopeful, but by the next day he was dead drunk again. He decided to enter Towns Hospital once again for treatment. Bill explains:

> ...I would go back to Towns Hospital where Dr. [William] Silkworth would sober me up again. Then I could look clear-eyed at Ebby's formula for sobriety. Perhaps I would not need an emotional conversion. Maybe a conservative doubter like me could get by without anything like that. Anyhow, I started for the hospital....
>
> Bright and early one morning friend Ebby showed up and stood in the doorway [of the hospital room], smiling broadly. I didn't see what was so funny. Then I had a suspicion: maybe this is the day he is going to evangelize me; maybe he is going to pour on the sweetness and light. But no, he made me wait until I asked him. "Well," said I, "what is your neat little formula once more?" In perfectly good humor, he handed it out again: You admit you are licked; you get honest with yourself; you talk it out with somebody else; you make restitution to the people you have harmed; you try to give of yourself with stint, with no demand for reward; and you pray to whatever God you think there is, even as an experiment. It was as simple and yet as mysterious as that. After some small talk he was gone.
>
> My depression deepened unbearably and finally it seemed to me as though I were at the very bottom of the pit. I still gagged badly on the notion of a Power greater than myself, but finally, just for the moment, the last vestige of my proud obstinacy was crushed. All at once I found myself crying out, "If there is a God, let Him show Himself! I am ready to do anything, anything!"

Suddenly the room lit up with a great white light. I was caught up into an ecstasy which there are no words to describe. It seemed to me, in the mind's eye, that I was on a mountain and that a wind not of air but of spirit was blowing. And then it burst upon me that I was a free man. Slowly the ecstasy subsided. I lay on the bed, but now for a time I was in another world, a new world of consciousness. All about me and through me there was a wonderful feeling of Presence....[6]

Business Trip Brings Temptation

With this newfound spiritual experience, it appeared as though Bill's drinking days were over. As soon as he was released from the hospital he began attending Oxford Group meetings, trying unsuccessfully to sober up other alcoholics.[7] Then, in May of 1935, although Bill had not had a drink for several months, a business trip to Akron, Ohio, resulted in a disaster, and the temptation to drink was great. As he was pacing back and forth in the lobby of the Mayflower Hotel, debating on whether to get drunk or not, an idea struck him. He thought that if he could talk to another alcoholic, perhaps he would be able to avoid his temptation for a drink.

While he thought about finding another alcoholic to whom he could talk, he saw a church directory in the lobby. At random, he chose an Episcopalian minister by the name of Walter Tunks. Placing a phone call to him, he asked him if he could give him a name of a member of the Oxford Group with whom to associate while in Akron. Although Tunks wasn't an Oxford Group member, he did know several people who were, so he gave Bill a list of about ten people.

Bill called the names on the list and one by one excuses were made. Near the end of the list was the name of Mrs. Henrietta ("Henry") Sieberling. He called Henry, another Oxford Group member, and she invited him over for lunch. During the course of conversation, she told him that she had just the right man for him to talk to. He was an Akron surgeon and an alcoholic whose name was Robert Smith.[8]

Robert Holbrook Smith, M.D. (August 8, 1879-November 16, 1950), son of Judge and Mrs. W. P. Smith, was born in St. Johnsbury, Vermont. In 1898 he graduated from St. Johnsbury Academy and then spent four years at Dartmouth College, graduating from there in 1902. Drinking became a major activity for him during these school years, but three years later when he entered the University of Michigan as a pre-med student, his drinking had increased. In spite of his drinking, he was able to pass his exams and in 1910 he earned his medical degree and began an internship at the City Hospital in Akron.

He married Anne Ripley in 1915, but his drinking only grew worse. In his desperation, he started to attend Oxford Group meetings in the early 1930's. Even though he had been attending for 2 1/2 years, he was still unable to stop his drinking. His medical practice was beginning to suffer because those who knew of his alcoholism were afraid to allow him to do surgery on them.

An Important Phone Call

One day in May of 1935, the Smiths' phone rang. It was Mrs. Sieberling asking Bob and Anne to come over to her home to meet an alcoholic who wanted to talk to another alcoholic. The next day Bob Smith met Bill Wilson. As the two men talked, Bob realized that they had a lot in common concerning their drinking problem. They talked for several hours and Bob was able to stop drinking immediately. However, a short while later, a medical conference was scheduled in Atlantic City and Bob went. It was during this convention that he got extremely drunk. Bill writes of this experience:

> We got Bob back home and into bed, and right then we made an alarming discovery. He had to perform a certain operation that only he could do. The deadline was just three days away; he simply had to do the job himself; and here he was, shaking like a leaf....

[Three days later] Anne and I drove him to the hospital at nine o'clock. I handed him a bottle of beer to steady his nerves so he could hold the knife, and he went in....That was June 10, 1935. To the time of his death fifteen years later, Dr. Bob never took another drink of alcohol.[9]

After Bob and Bill were sobered up, they started to work to rescue other alcoholics from their drinking problems, and Alcoholics Anonymous was born. Of course, AA was not known by this name at first.[10] AA, at this point, was working alongside, and in association with, the Oxford Group.[11] By June 1935, Bill had been a member of the Oxford Group in New York for six or seven months while Dr. Bob had already been attending their meetings in Akron for 2 1/2 years.[12] Mrs. Sieberling, the woman who introduced the two men, and Ebby, the man who was responsible for helping Bill achieve sobriety, were also associated with Oxford Groups. Since these people were all Oxford Group members, let's see if the Oxford Group had any influence on the newly-formed group of ex- alcoholics. If so, who started the Oxford Group, what did the Oxford Group teach, and what role did it play in the founding of Alcoholics Anonymous? This part of the history of AA never seems to be discussed in detail, but it is significantly important if we are to fully understand AA and its Twelve Steps and Twelve Traditions. In the next chapter we will begin to explore and uncover a little of the background of the Oxford Group and its founder, Frank Buchman.

2. WHO IS
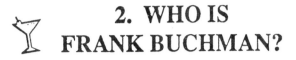
FRANK BUCHMAN?

Frank Nathan Daniel Buchman, a German, was born on June 4, 1878, in Pennsburg, Pennsylvania.[1] After graduating in 1902 from Mount Airy Lutheran Seminary in Philadelphia, he served as a Lutheran pastor in that town where he combined his pastoral duties with social work. In 1908, Buchman attended the Keswick Conference in England and claimed to have had a "conversion experience."[2]

Buchman seems to have run into trouble time and again in his lifetime. While in Philadelphia, a dispute came up with the trustees of a youth hostel run by him. This difference between them resulted in Buchman's resignation.

> Later he worked successfully as secretary of the college Young Men's Christian association (sic) at Pennsylvania State university (sic), which led to his appointment as lecturer in personal evangelism at the Hartford Seminary foundation (sic) at Hartford, Conn., and also to evangelistic work, mostly among college students. Following friction at Hartford he resigned in 1922 to "live by faith" and launch a world-wide evangelistic campaign based on God's guidance, moral absolutes and the "life-changing" of individuals through personal work. The centre of Buchman's operations was shifted to the campus of Princeton university (sic), where he encountered even sharper opposition and where the authorities finally asked him in 1926 to cease his work. Subsequently he was successful in winning influential support at Oxford university (sic), and the movement gradually became known as the Oxford Group (not to be confused with the Oxford Movement).[3]

The Oxford Group, which Buchman founded in 1921, was originally called the First Century Christian Fellowship.[4] The name "Oxford Group" was not used until 1929 in South Africa when a railway porter:

... scribbled the phrase on labels stuck on the windows of the reserved compartments in which a team of Buchmanites [another name for Buchman's group]—mostly, as it happened, from Oxford, some being Rhodes Scholars—were travelling. The South African press picked up the tag and the Buchmanites (as one of their supporters was to put it, much later) "submitted to the appellation."[5]

In 1938, the name was once again changed—this time to Moral Rearmament or MRA.[6]

Oxford Group's Beliefs

Just what is the Oxford Group and what did it teach? The Oxford Group

... has no churches and no pastors. It is not a denomination, but a worldwide spiritual fellowship. Buchman taught that a man could begin quietly each day with pen and paper and write down the impressions and instructions from "God," whomever that may be for the individual. This was called Quiet Time.[7]

The tenets of the group rest on four absolutes: Absolute Honesty, Absolute Purity, Absolute Unselfishness, and Absolute Love.[8]

The "house parties" actually started in China as early as 1918, and gradually grew into the Oxford Group, which was then called the First Century Christian Fellowship.[9] This theory of "Guidance," which is central to the belief of the Oxford Group, was first practiced by Frank Buchman while he was at Penn State. He had decided to spend one ho⁻ ⌐ry morning from five to six o'clock "listening in to the orders of the day." These orders were supposed to come from God, who would wake him up every morning to tell Buchman what he was supposed to know for the day.[10] This practice was carried over into the group founded by him. The Buchmanites would sit with pencil and paper during what was called their "Quiet Time" and would then write down any thoughts that would come to them. Here is a description of one of these quiet times by an eye-witness account of a former Oxford Group member:

> The team is sitting in a semi-circle around Sam. "Well," Sam asks, "what's the plan for to-night's meeting? Let's listen."... "Guidance-books" appear, pencils fly swiftly over blank sheets. Some peer glassily at the ceiling. Others close their eyes momentarily, and are invariably rewarded with two or three lines of guidance. "Amen. What comes?", Sam asks, as the scrape of pencils and pens perceptibly diminishes in volume, thereby indicating to him that the details of God's plan had been fully communicated. Sharing begins. "Any guidance about the motif?" "It comes to me that J. ought to give a good wad on Sin. My guidance is that we shall get the pious crowd to-night," says B. "That checks with my guidance," says another. "Check," "check," "check," echoes from many of the team. "That's it, Sin—that's what I got too. Sin is the drive for to-night." (It should be noted that guidance is regarded as being practically infallible when a majority is in agreement.) The door opens. Frank [Buchman] walks in, and sits next to Sam. "How far have you got with to-night's meeting?", he asks. "It seems clear that sin is the motif to-night," Sam tells him. Frank interrupts quickly: "Now wait a minute. I'm not so sure. I've got a feeling that it may be too early for sin. "Intrigue" is what came to me in my early quiet time. You've got to get hold of that important pagan bunch. Play with 'em—show 'em what they're missing. Give 'em the feeling that religion's more fun than cocktail parties. Suppose we have further Quiet, and check up on it."
>
> More Quiet. More writing. Frank was always a tonic. Every one writes more busily. Guidance comes more easily. The words "intrigue" and "hilarity" appear on many notebooks. "Amen, what comes!", asks Frank. "I got 'intrigue' this time," says B. Sam seemed to have got different guidance too this time. (The phrases "right guidance" and "bad guidance" were in common use.) "I check with you, Frank," he says. "It came to me that I must be more flexible, and have no preconceptions." "Check," "check," "check," again echoes round the room. Frank resumes. "Well now, I'll share my guidance—A battery of witness from

young Oxford. They want to hear Oxford, so we'll let 'em. Crisp nuggets of witness. Intrigue the young pagan elements. Sweep 'em along. That's my guidance. Now I don't want to dictate. I may be wrong. I want you to check me." But we knew better. Frank's guidance was always right.[11]

"Guidance" Sessions Bring Surprises

It should be obvious by this account that Buchman did not practice what he preached. His tenet of Absolute Unselfishness certainly didn't seem to apply to his OWN life, as he was determined to have his own way. It should also be evident that he held a tremendous power of influence over his group members. Notice how quickly the "Guidance" these people had obtained could be changed to agree with that of their leader. Was the Guidance they were receiving actually coming from God or was Buchman the one in control, or was someone or something else in control? Actually, *SOMEONE INVISIBLE* was showing up at these house parties and quiet times. Texe Marrs relates:

> Evidently, it wasn't "God" alone who always visited Buchman's disciples. Word began to spread that members of the various Oxford Group chapters that had sprung up in Britain, the United States, and elsewhere were getting together for Quiet Time "Spook Parties" and that bizarre spirits from beyond made their presence known. Guidance from these spirits was certainly unorthodox and rumors began to be heard that some groups were involved in sexual misconduct.[12]

Guidance from spirits also came through A. J. Russell. Russell, a disciple of Frank Buchman, wrote a book entitled *For Sinners Only*. In this book, considered to be "scriptures" for the Buchmanites,[13] he "reveals experiences with spirit beings whom he could not identify. These spirit beings, he admits, told him what to write and how and where to get his writings published."[14] Russell, writing in *For Sinners Only*, mentions about some Guidance he received during one session. The impact of this Guidance was so impressive to him that he put the entire paragraph in italics. He comments:

Then suddenly a flash came to show me that this book was to be written, followed by another giving me the title. I sat up startled!... "That checks. It rings a bell," was the opinion expressed by Ray Purdy immediately I began to tell him what was in my mind. The urge had come not as a strong luminous thought or a soundless whisper in the atmosphere, but as sudden pressure on my brain. [Emphasis in the original.][15]

This Guidance, however, wasn't always so insightful. "In one instance, Russell describes a demonic force that attacked and entered him while he lay helplessly paralyzed on his bed."[16]

Another feature of the Oxford Group was their technique which was called Sharing. This practice consisted of confessing one's sins to another member of the group or sometimes to the entire group. This procedure is contrary to Biblical teaching where we are told that "there is ONE mediator between God and men, the man Christ Jesus" (I Timothy 2:15). Confessing our sins to another person is not sufficient and will never cleanse us of those sins which we have committed.

One of the four absolutes that helps build the foundation of the Oxford Group is absolute purity. How did Buchman's life add up in this area? Well, it was rumored that he was a homosexual.[17] We are also told:

A Harvard law-student, describing a "house-party" in the *American* on 20th October, 1926, quoted a graduate who was also present as having said to him, of Buchman: "He started asking me intimate questions about sex before I'd been alone with him for five minutes. I left in a hurry."[18]

"Thank God for Hitler"

As far as another principle, Absolute Love, Buchman ranks higher than most people. In fact, he had a great love for one particular person—Adolf Hitler! "In 1936 Buchman stated, 'I thank God for a man like Adolf Hitler,' apparently because he thought a dictator, if he listened to God, could bring about the millennium."[19] This statement praising Hitler appeared in numerous newspapers across America, including *Time, Newsweek*,[20] and *New York World-Telegram*.[21] Buchman furthermore remarked about Hitler's accommodation to the Oxford Group: "He lets us have house-parties whenever we like."[22]

> It was also revealed that Buchman had traveled to Germany on a secret mission to meet with Heinrich Himmler, head of the Nazi concentration camps and joint architect of Hitler's grandiose scheme for a One World Religion (*Societas Satana*) planned once the predicted Nazi world conquest had succeeded.[23]

While in Berlin, Buchman talked with Mr. Kenneth Lindsay, MP for Kilmarnock Burghs and a member of the British Government. Buchman asked Lindsay if he knew Heinrich Himmler and when Lindsay answered in the negative, Buchman responded: "Say, you ought to know Heinrich. He's a great lad."[24] Buchman most likely had been aware that Himmler was the head of the Gestapo, which was a secret police force already recognized for its brutality.[25]

Buchman could hardly have been ignorant about Hitler's regime because Hitler was in authority for three years and the West already knew about his oppression. Buchman himself revealed in the interview that appeared in the *New York World-Telegram* that he was aware of the Jewish people being persecuted because in his adulation for Hitler he let it be known that he was glad for the Nazis' efforts against the Jews.[26]

Absolute honesty is yet another discipline of the Oxford Group, but again Buchman falls short of his teaching. Numerous examples could be given but one instance should suffice. In his notation in *Who's Who* he lists his educational summary as follows: "Muhlenberg College, AB, AM, DD, LLD (Oglethorpe), studied Cambridge University, 1921-22."[27] The problem is, however, that Buchman never did study at Cambridge.[28] For a man who preached absolute honesty, he certainly did not measure up to his guidelines.

Having explained some of Buchman's history and the group he organized, you are probably wondering just how all this fits into Alcoholics Anonymous. If you remember in the last chapter, we discovered that the co-founders of AA, Bill Wilson and Bob Smith, were both Oxford Group members when AA was launched. Also, the lady who introduced the two men, Mrs. Henrietta Seiberling, belonged to this fellowship. Just how much of the Oxford Group's influence carried over into the founding of AA? Let's look at this issue in the next chapter.

 3. THE OXFORD GROUP'S LEGACY

If someone belongs to a certain group, organization, or fellowship at the time of forming another group, does that mean that the new group will have many of the same ideas and practices of the old group? Of course not. Many times this is true, but there are also occasions when a clean break is made from a former group and no further connections are maintained. So, did co-founders Bill Wilson and Bob Smith carry the philosophies of the Oxford Group into Alcoholics Anonymous? If not, how did AA differ from the Oxford Group? If, on the other hand, the practices were disseminated into AA, what ideas, values, beliefs, and doctrines were maintained? Let's look at the literature from AA so that we can be as fair as possible.

The *A. A. Fact File,* prepared by the General Service Office of Alcoholics Anonymous, the AA headquarters in New York, mentions the Oxford Group under the heading of "Historical Data." They state:

A.A. had its beginnings in 1935 at Akron, Ohio, as the outcome of a meeting between Bill W. [Wilson], a New York stockbroker, and Dr. Bob S. [Smith], an Akron surgeon. Both had been hopeless alcoholics.

Prior to that time, Bill and Dr. Bob had each been in contact with the Oxford Group, a mostly nonalcoholic fellowship that emphasized universal spiritual values in daily living. In that period, the Oxford Groups in America were headed by the noted Episcopal clergyman Dr. Samuel Shoemaker. Under this spiritual influence, and with the help of an old-time friend, Ebby T., Bill had sobered and had then maintained his recovery by working with other alcoholics, though none of these had actually recovered. Meanwhile, Dr. Bob's Oxford Group membership at Akron had not helped him enough to achieve sobriety.[1]

A Landmark in AA's History

Even though the Oxford Group is mentioned in this book, there's no conclusive proof here that AA patterned their new organization after the Oxford Group. It simply states that these men were Oxford Group members. However, let's look at another AA book entitled *Alcoholics Anonymous Comes of Age*. On page vii there is a section headed as "Landmarks in A.A. History." The word "landmark" means "highlight" or "milestone," "a distinguishing feature." What events are significant and important to AA? One landmark listed was in August 1934 when the Oxford Groups sobered up Ebby T. Another landmark was in 1937 when the New York AA's separated from the Oxford Groups. Yet another landmark noted was in the Summer of 1939 when the Midwest AA's withdrew from the Oxford Groups and were able to finally be on their own.[2]

Alcoholics Anonymous consider the date of their founding to be the day that Dr. Bob Smith sobered up, which was June 10, 1935.[3] A little mathematical calculation tells us that from June 10, 1935, until the New York AA's broke away in 1937, was approximately two years. So, for about two years Alcoholics Anonymous was actually under the banner of the Oxford Groups! In fact, the final breakaway was not until four years later.

Although this AA book lists the founding of its organization on June 10, 1935, this is not the full truth. In 1938 (three years after the so-called founding of AA), the group still did not have a name. What happened was this: There were a number of alcoholics who had achieved sobriety and so they thought that they would put their testimonies into a book. While they were discussing a title for the book, the name *Alcoholics Anonymous* was suggested. A lot of the members did not want this title. The title that many desired was *The Way Out*. Because of this controversy, one member checked out the titles of books already printed. They found that 12 other books were entitled *The Way Out*, but none were named *Alcoholics Anonymous*.

Not wanting their book to be the 13th one named *The Way Out*, an agreement was quickly reached to entitle it *Alcoholics Anonymous*. This was the first that the name was used! In fact, the SAME BOOK that states that AA was founded June 10, 1935 also informs us:

> The title "Alcoholics Anonymous" had appeared very early in the discussion [of the book], probably in October, 1938. We do not know who first used these words. After we New Yorkers had left the Oxford Groups in 1937 we often described ourselves as a "nameless bunch of alcoholics." From this phrase it was only a step to the idea of "Alcoholics Anonymous." This was its actual derivation.[4]

Did you notice the sentence which states: "AFTER we New Yorkers had left the Oxford Group in 1937 we often described ourselves as a 'NAMELESS bunch of alcoholics?'" [Emphasis added.] In other words, until 1937, the New York AA's were known as an Oxford Group and AFTER they left this group, they were "NAMELESS" or without a name of their own until sometime after late 1938.

A Mixed Bunch

In the book *Alcoholics Anonymous* is the testimony of the one man who joined AA in 1939, after he was released from City Hospital. This individual describes the meetings he attended like this:

> I did not know there was such a thing as group activity until I left the hospital. I left on a Wednesday afternoon, had dinner in Akron and then went to a house where I encountered my first meeting. I had attended several of these meetings before I discovered that all those who were there were not alcoholics. That is, it was sort of a mixed bunch of Oxford Groupers, who were interested in the alcoholic problem, and of alcoholics themselves.[5]

Did you notice that Oxford Group members and the alcoholics were a "mixed bunch?" In other words, the Oxford Groupers and the

AAs were working side by side and intermingling with each other. So, we have now discovered that the AA and the Oxford Group were actually connected to each other for a number of years. What caused the final break and how did the AA members feel about leaving the Oxford Group? Did they leave because they could not agree with the Oxford Group's philosophy? Were they embarrassed over Frank Buchman's endorsement of Adolf Hitler? Here is how the AA literature recounts this separation:

> Until the middle of 1937 we in New York had been working alongside the Oxford Groups. But in the latter part of that year we **MOST RELUCTANTLY PARTED COMPANY** with these **GREAT FRIENDS**....

> The Oxford Groupers had clearly shown us what to do. And, just as importantly, we had also learned from them *what not to do* as far as alcoholics were concerned. We had found that certain of their ideas and attitudes simply could not be sold to alcoholics. For example, drinkers would not take pressure in any form, excepting from John Barleycorn itself. They always had to be led, not pushed. They would not stand for the rather aggressive evangelism of the Oxford Groups. And they would not accept the principle of "team guidance" for their own personal lives. It was too authoritarian for them....

> The Oxford Groups' absolute concepts—absolute purity, absolute honesty, absolute unselfishness, and absolute love— were frequently too much for the drunks. These ideas had to be fed with teaspoons rather than by buckets....

> There was yet another difficulty. Because of the stigma then attached to the condition, most alcoholics wanted to be anonymous. We were afraid also of developing erratic public characters who, through broken anonymity, might get drunk in public and so destroy confidence in us. The Oxford Groups, on the contrary, depended very much upon the use of prominent names—something that was doubtless all right for them but mighty hazardous for us. OUR DEBT TO THEM, nevertheless, WAS AND IS IMMENSE, and so **THE FINAL BREAKAWAY**

WAS VERY PAINFUL. [Italics in the original; Bold and capitals added.][6]

AA Adopts Oxford Groups Tenets

I believe that it should be clear from the above quotations that Alcoholics Anonymous and the Oxford Groups were closely aligned—so closely aligned that the break was "VERY PAINFUL." Even when the separation did come, it was not for reasons of disagreement with the principles and beliefs that the Oxford Group held. This split was one year after Buchman's applause of Hitler, but nothing about this statement is mentioned or retracted. There is only praise for the Oxford Group and its principles. By the way, did you notice how the AA literature approved of the tenets of the group? The book states that the four absolute concepts were oftentimes "too much for the drunks," and because of that, they had to feed the ideas to the alcoholics in "teaspoons rather than by buckets." Even though the dose was lowered in AA circles, the same concepts were being applied. In fact, this book from AA explains:

> The basic principles which the Oxford Groupers had taught were ancient and universal ones, the common property of mankind....
>
> But the important thing is this: the early A.A. got its ideas of self-examination, acknowledgement of character defects, restitution for harm done, and working with others straight from the Oxford Groups and directly from Sam Shoemaker, their former leader in America, and from **NOWHERE ELSE.** He will always be found in our annals as the one whose inspired example and teaching did most to show us how to create the spiritual climate in which we alcoholics may survive and then proceed to grow. [Emphasis added.][7]

Sam Shoemaker is held in high esteem in the sight of the two AA co-founders. Bill Wilson comments that it was Shoemaker's teachings that inspired both Dr. Bob and him.[8] Bill further adds:

It was from him [Sam Shoemaker] that Dr. Bob and I in the beginning had absorbed most of the principles that were afterward embodied in the Twelve Steps of Alcoholics Anonymous, steps that express the heart of A.A.'s way of life. Dr. [William] Silkworth gave us the needed knowledge of our illness but Sam Shoemaker had given us the concrete knowledge of what we could do about it. One showed us the mysteries of the lock that held us in prison; the other passed on the spiritual keys by which we were liberated.[9]

Shoemaker was even invited as a guest speaker at AA's 20th anniversary celebration.

How close was Sam Shoemaker to Frank Buchman, the man who praised Adolf Hitler? Actually, they were quite close!

For some years Mr (sic) Shoemaker was the **MOST PROMINENT** of the American clergy and ministers identified with the Buchman Group. He was Rector of Calvary Church in New York, and his parochial mission house was used as MRA's [Moral Rearmament, the name to which the Oxford Group was changed in 1938] national headquarters. As such, it was frequently the scene of characteristic Buchmanite gatherings. [Emphasis added.][10]

Since Shoemaker had such a tremendous impact on the principles embodied in the Twelve Steps of Alcoholics Anonymous, we will turn our attention to what these steps actually teach in the next chapter, but first let's take a look at why Bill Wilson attended Shoemaker's Calvary Church. It was during Bill Wilson's 1935 extended summer visit at Bob Smith's home that the OCCULT activities of Bob and Bill became evident, although this curiosity in the occult went back many years before the founding of AA. One book tells us that Wilson, alcoholics, and homeless men would gather at the Calvary Church's mission for lectures on SPIRITUALISM! We also know that when Bill Wilson married Lois Burnham in 1918 he was already interested in occultism. You see, Lois' grandfather was a minister in the Swedenborgian Church, also known as the New Church or the Church of the New Jerusalem. The founder of the Swedenborgian Church was Emmanuel Swedenborg. He practiced automatic writing and astral travel. Bill knew of the Burnhams' involvement in this OCCULT group and he and Lois vowed to explore it more deeply some day. In fact, they were even married in the Swedenborgian Church in Brooklyn, New York.

Both Dr. Bob and Bill were involved with all kinds of psychic phenomena such as ESP, seances, spiritualism, necromancy, which is communication with the dead, and channeling. Bill was so proficient and told him their names! On one occasion alone, at least SIX different entities came through him. The Bible clearly tells us in numerous passages such as Deuteronomy 18:10-12 that those who do such things are an abomination unto the Lord. Galatians 5:19-21 informs us that those who practice occultism cannot enter heaven. Bill also believed in reincarnation, precognition, clairvoyance and used an ouija board.

Dr. Bob read books on voodooism and in 1935, when AA was started, Bob and Bill were holding seances and other psychic events, and as early as 1941, Bill and Lois were holding regular Saturday "spook sessions." They even had the one bedroom dubbed the "spook room."

In *Pass It On*, a book APPROVED by the AA headquarters in New York, we find this quotation: "'They [meaning Dr. Bob and Bill] were working away at the spiritualism; it was not just a hobby. AND IT RELATED TO AA.... So the thing WAS NOT at all divorced from AA.'...Bill never did anything that was not in some way CONNECTED WITH AA and with his own spiritual growth."[11]

In a book entitled *Lois Remembers*, written by Bill's wife, Lois, she tells us that "...Bill and I and some of our neighboring AA friends became interested in extrasensory perception [ESP] and used to meet every Saturday night to experiment. Much enlightenment was gained by all. Bill, as usual when his interest was aroused, became absorbed in the subject and could talk of nothing else—except, of course, AA.[12]

In this book by Lois is an intriguing picture of the Christmas card Bill and she sent out in 1970. It shows them sitting by their fireplace and on the wall is a huge pentagram. This is a very important symbol to witches, Masons, occultists, and Satanists. Just a month after this card was sent out, Bill died, so we see he was involved in the occult right up to his death.

Bill was also very interested in and read books on Christian Science and the New Thought movement and he said that we must in all things turn to "the father of light." This is a phrase referring to Lucifer, the Light bearer and II Corinthians 11:14 tells us that Satan (or Lucifer) comes as an "angel of light."

This occultic exploration is still prevalent in many AA groups today. When I called the AA headquarters and asked how they felt about ESP, visions, meditation, and other pyschic phenomena, I was told that AA is very open to all kinds of phenomena like that!

So, from AA's own books and words we can see how prevalent the occult was in the lives of AA's co-founders—before, during, and after the founding of AA. In fact, the Twelve Step programs appear to have been written while Bill was in a trance state! In other words, the Steps which are the foundation upon which AA is built, were produced through automatic writing which is an occult practice used by spirit mediums. We will now turn our attention to these 12 Steps in the next chapter.

4. GOD—AS *YOU* UNDERSTAND HIM

The philosophy of Alcoholics Anonymous can be summed up in their Twelve Steps and the Twelve Traditions. These steps are:

1. We admitted we were powerless over alcohol—that our lives had become unmanageable.

2. Came to believe that a Power greater than ourselves could restore us to sanity.

3. Made a decision to turn our will and our lives over to the care of God, *as we understood Him.*

4. Made a searching and fearless moral inventory of ourselves.

5. Admitted to God, to ourselves, and to another human being the exact nature of our wrongs.

6. Were entirely ready to have God remove all these defects of character.

7. Humbly asked Him to remove our shortcomings.

8. Made a list of all persons we had harmed, and became willing to make amends to them all.

9. Made direct amends to such people wherever possible, except when to do so would injure them or others.

10. Continued to take personal inventory and when we were wrong promptly admitted it.

11. Sought through prayer and meditation to improve our conscious contact with God *as we understood Him,* praying only for knowledge of His will for us and the power to carry that out.

12. Having had a spiritual awakening as the result of these steps, we tried to carry this message to alcoholics and to practice these principles in all our affairs.[1]

If you gave a superficial glance at the above steps, you may think they look good. After all, doesn't Christianity teach some of the same ideas? Don't Christians believe in restitution, prayer, God, a spiritual awakening, and confession? Yes, we do, but if these steps are looked at in closer detail, many problems start to arise. First of all, AA's terminology is different and has ANOTHER meaning than what Bible-believing Christians accept. Notice that instead of saying that the alcoholic has committed sin, it is only called "defects of character" or a "shortcoming." AA does not consider drinking alcoholic beverages wrong; it is only "wrong" for those who become alcoholics.

Confession—AA-Style

AA believes in confession ("Admitted to God, to ourselves, and to another human being the exact nature of our wrongs."), but again confession has a different meaning. In the Oxford Group, from which we have seen that these principles have emanated, confession consisted of telling your wrongs to another person or the group. It was a public type of confession, but it had nothing to do with the confessing of a person's sins to God and asking for His forgiveness. It was sort of a catharsis for an individual or a means by which to relieve a guilty conscience, but relieving a guilty conscience is not the same thing as having your sins forgiven by the atonement of Christ on the cross.

There are many instances in the Bible where people "confessed" their sins, but confession ALONE is not enough. One example would be Pharaoh. After the seventh plague was poured out upon Egypt, Pharaoh called in Moses and Aaron and said: "I HAVE SINNED this time: the Lord is righteous, and I and my people are wicked. Intreat the Lord (for it is enough) that there be no more mighty thunderings and hail; and I will let you go, and ye shall stay no longer" (Exodus

9:27-28). Here we find that Pharaoh made a confession by saying "I HAVE SINNED." Did this confession save him? No, for as soon as the plague was stopped, Pharaoh once again hardened his heart and would not let the children of Israel go as he had promised. It seems as though Pharaoh only admitted that he had sinned because he wanted the plagues stopped. He had no real intention of keeping his promise. There are many who are in pressing circumstances and facing death who will cry out, "Lord, if You will spare my life, I will serve You," but as soon as they are up and on their feet again, the promise that they made is forgotten. CONFESSION was made, but there was NO TRUE REPENTANCE.

Other people who confessed that they had sinned (but who did not repent of their sins and ask for forgiveness) are: Achan (Joshua 7:20), King Saul (I Samuel 15:24-25), Balaam (Numbers 22:34), and Judas, the betrayer of Jesus (Matthew 27:4). The Bible, on the other hand, also records a couple of instances in which people did confess their sins and repent of them, and where forgiveness was extended. One such example is King David. David, after committing adultery with Bathsheba, admitted that he had sinned (II Samuel 12:13) and the Lord forgave Him. David not only confessed his sin but he also prayed:

> Have mercy upon me, O God... blot out my transgressions. Wash me throughly from mine iniquity, and cleanse me from my sin. For I acknowledge my transgressions: and my sin is ever before me. Against Thee, Thee only, have I sinned, and done this evil in Thy sight.... Create in me a clean heart, O God; and renew a right spirit within me. Cast me not away from Thy presence; and take not Thy holy spirit from me. Restore unto me the joy of Thy salvation; and uphold me with Thy free spirit (Psalm 51:1-12, in part).

We can see that David not only made a CONFESSION to God (and not to others only), but he truly REPENTED of his sin.

Results of True Repentance

There are several things that take place when sin is confessed and repented of:

1. Your sins are blotted out—"I have blotted out, as a thick cloud, thy transgressions, and, as a cloud, thy sins…" (Isaiah 44:22).

2. Your sins are forgiven—"If we confess our sins, He is faithful and just to forgive us our sins, and to cleanse us from all unrighteousness" (I John 1:9).

3. Your sins are forgotten—"For I will be merciful to their unrighteousness, and their sins and their iniquities will I remember no more" (Hebrews 8:12).

4. Your sins are covered—"Blessed is he whose transgression is forgiven, whose sin is covered [by the blood of Christ]" (Psalm 32:1).

5. Your sins are washed away—"Unto Him that loved us, and washed us from our sins in His own blood" (Revelation 1:5).

6. Your sins are taken away—"And ye know that He was manifested to take away our sins; and in Him is no sin" (I John 3:5).

7. One is saved from sins—"And she shall bring forth a son, and thou shalt call His name Jesus: for He shall save His people from their sins" (Matthew 1:21).

8. One becomes dead to sins—"Who His own self bare our sins in His own body on the tree, that we, being dead to sins, should live unto righteousness: by whose stripes ye were healed" (I Peter 2:24).

These benefits, received only through Christ, can never be attained through confession to a group or to another individual. Let's not settle for a cheap counterfeit that may soothe our guilty conscience for a while, but let's get honest before God and make a real confession where we can receive full and complete forgiveness of the sins we have committed.

Group Confession

The Oxford Group, like AA, relies on a group confession. One author mentions this about Buchman and his form of confession:

> He tried to reach the well-to-do and educated through his gospel of the changed life, "sharing" or CONFESSION TO THE GROUP, guidance, and the four absolutes of honesty, purity, love and unselfishness. House parties for personal witnessing and PUBLIC CONFESSION have been the method of operation adopted by the group.... Two weaknesses of the Group are that the lack of a sound theology may lead to the substitution of the feeling of release, after one has "shared" sins, for real regeneration, and confession may be directed only to man rather than to God. [Emphasis added.][2]

Another source notes:

> The Oxford Group has many interesting psychological angles. Basically its appeal stems from the individual's feelings of guilt and anxiety. CONFESSION IN THE CHARACTERISTIC SMALL GROUP OF FOLLOWERS BRINGS RELIEF AND A FEELING OF UNITY WITH THE GROUP and with the larger movement.... Cantril notes that Buchmanism flourished in the depression years of the 1930's and took a spurt in the fall of 1938 when war was impending. He concluded as follows:

> "Buchmanism has gathered momentum, therefore, essentially because it shows certain bewildered people a way to interpret their personal troubles and the larger social problems of their world without endangering their status. It provides a psychological mechanism whereby they can escape the responsibility of dealing directly with conditions which they realize are not right and just. It attracts to itself people who want

to improve these conditions without injuring their own positions
and who want to avoid any alignment with existing institutions
or ideologies which assume that individual problems CANNOT
BE SOLVED WITHOUT COLLETIVE ACTION....

ONE OF ITS MOST EFFECTIVE MEANS OF GROUP
SHARING IS WITH ITS CONFESSIONALS WHICH
RECALL THE METHODS OF ALCOHOLICS ANONY-
MOUS." [Emphasis added.][3]

AA Brings a Spiritual Awakening

Step Twelve states that a **SPIRITUAL AWAKENING** is the
result of following the other eleven steps.[4] When AA mentions a
"spiritual awakening" and a "Higher Power," as it FREQUENTLY
does in its literature, what is meant by those terms? Wanda Marrs
informs us:

AA, Al-Anon, the Adult Children of Alcoholics, and other
twelve step programs have bought fully the New Age doctrines
of the Higher Self, integration, psychosynthesis and individuation,
as defined by Carl Jung and other occultists.

For example, in the book *Guide to Recovery*, a guide for
Adult Children of Alcoholics, authors Herbert Gravitz and Julie
Bowden discuss the concept of the Higher Self. They explain
that a higher level of consciousness is attained through one's
Higher Self.

Moreover, they state that the CHIEF GOAL of Alcoholics
Anonymous is to assist the individual to become whole—to
become one—with the Higher Self. This is, they say, the pathway
to "spiritual evolution." Those who walk the path of the twelve
step programs of Alcoholics Anonymous, Al-Anon, Overeaters
Anonymous, and so forth travel the "spiritual road" which
assures a "genesis" or an "awakening":

"Genesis (rebirth) is... the SPIRITUAL AWAKENING
spoken of in Alcoholics Anonymous; you begin to be aware of

a spiritual connection which unites us all in a sense of being one with the universe."

Keep in mind that AA's "spiritual awakening" does not make you a Christian, nor does a 12-stepper have to believe in and accept Jesus as Lord. According to AA and other twelve step programs, the healed and spiritually mature person "awakens" to her oneness with the universe. This is New Age religion *par excellence*. It is union with the spirit of the Goddess, which AA prefers to describe as connecting with one's "higher power" or "god as you understand him." [Italics in the original; Capitals added.][5]

AA's "Higher Power"

Is AA as bad as it really sounds? After all, they frequently have references about a "Higher Power " and "God." Can you believe in God and still be influenced by the New Age philosophy? Again, we have to look at what AA actually means when they refer to God. They certainly DO NOT speak of the God of the Bible, although many people believe this is what is intended. Rather, AA recommends a "God as YOU understand Him." It doesn't matter whether you believe a supernatural being or the AA group itself is your "God" or "Higher Power." For proof, let's look at a few quotations from AA's own books, APPROVED BY THE ALCOHOLIC ANONYMOUS HEADQUARTERS.

1. Some clergymen may be shocked to learn that an agnostic or atheist may join the Fellowship, or to hear an A.A. member say: "I can't accept that 'God concept'; I put my faith in THE A.A. GROUP; THAT'S MY HIGHER POWER, and it keeps me sober!" [Emphasis added.][6]

2. Most members, before turning to A.A., had already admitted that they could not control their drinking. Alcohol had become a power greater than themselves [here alcohol is a "Higher Power"!], and it had been accepted on those terms. A.A. suggests that to achieve and maintain sobriety, alcoholics need

to accept and depend upon **ANOTHER POWER** recognized as greater than themselves. SOME ALCOHOLICS CHOOSE TO CONSIDER THE A.A. GROUP ITSELF AS THE POWER GREATER THAN THEMSELVES; for many others, this Power is God—*as they, individually, understand Him*; still others rely upon entirely different concepts of a Higher Power. [Italics in the original; Bold and capitals added.][7]

3. The majority of A.A. members believe that we have found the solution to our drinking problem not through individual willpower, but through a power greater than ourselves. However, EVERYONE DEFINES THIS POWER AS HE OR SHE WISHES. Many people call it God, others think IT IS THE A.A. GROUP, still others don't believe in it at all. There is room in A.A. for people of all shades of belief and nonbelief. [Emphasis added.][8]

4. For a long time the only Higher Power I could concede was the power of the group, but this was far more than I had ever recognized before, and it was at least a beginning.[9]

5. [In response to an argument that could be presented by an atheist, a sponsor replies:] "I must quickly assure you that AA's tread INNUMERABLE PATHS IN THEIR QUEST FOR FAITH. If you don't care for the one I've suggested, you'll be sure to discover one that suits if only you look and listen. Many a man like you had begun to solve the problem by the method of substitution. YOU CAN, IF YOU WISH, MAKE A.A. ITSELF YOUR 'HIGHER POWER.' Here's a very large group of people who have solved their alcohol problem. In this respect they are certainly a power greater than you, who have not even come close to a solution. Surely you can have faith in them. Even this minimum of faith will be enough...." For the time being, WE WHO WERE ATHEIST OR AGNOSTIC DISCOVERED THAT OUR OWN GROUP, OR A.A. AS A WHOLE, WOULD SUFFICE AS A HIGHER POWER. [Emphasis added.][10]

Many other examples could be given, but you can easily see that the "Higher Power" in AA can be ANYONE or ANYTHING. An article in one journal goes into greater detail on this point:

> The Higher Power—like spirituality—is a generic but highly personalized concept that bypasses all the biases and defenses alcoholics may have concerning God and religion. A HIGHER POWER IS SIMPLY **ANYTHING OR ANYBODY** that guides, directs, motivates, controls, and gives meaning and purpose to one's life.
>
> With this BROAD DEFINITION in mind, the alcoholic cannot not but have a higher power, regardless of his or her religious background or lack of it. Simply put, everyone—including the alcoholic—has a god, even if it is spelled with a little g. HIGHER POWERS CAN ASSUME MANY FORMS, but come in two basic types: those that confine, control, punish and shame, and those that give permission to risk, grow, forgive, and let go of guilt and shame.
>
> A list of dysfunctional Higher Powers would include all compulsive behaviors from substance abuse to gambling, materialism, workaholism, codependent relationships, and a punitive God concept. Examples of positive, healthy Higher Powers would include support and recovery groups—religious or otherwise—and would certainly include a more gracious, forgiving God concept. [Emphasis added.][11]

Terminology Different

The terminology "Higher Power" makes the average person think of God, but as has been illustrated, this "Higher Power" does not necessarily include a supernatural God. Even when God is alluded to, it is a "God as YOU understand Him," not as He is presented in the Bible. The sad part is that many religious leaders are buying into this idea that the "Higher Power" in AA is the same as the God of the Bible. For example, a prominent psychologist had four guests on his radio program who discussed and praised the AA philosophy and mentioned that the "Higher Power" reference in AA pointed individuals to Jesus in an **"INDIRECT WAY."**[12]

Two writers, commenting on this particular program, explain that the radio host seems to consider

> ... A.A. to be a possible evangelistic tool since it recognizes a "Higher Power." However, we would like to say that while God is sovereign and He can save a person in any circumstance of life, including a bar or a brothel, A.A. is not a place that is conducive to that. A.A. meetings are filled with smoke, swearing, and sexual contacts. The main focus is ceasing from substance abuse but almost any other sin is permissible. The introduction of a higher power is less than meaningless. It can even be dangerous because the higher power can be any false god, including a "higher self" or Satan. All are acceptable to A.A.[13]

This program ended with the announcer remarking that a fact sheet could be obtained through this radio ministry. The fact sheet listed steps on how to start a support group with a notation that stated that the "information provided in this booklet has been mainly adapted from AA materials and concepts" and that "The 12 Steps to Healing... were modified from the Alcoholics Anonymous 12 Steps."[14] As mentioned in the last chapter, the Twelve Steps of AA were derived from the Oxford Group. Although some who promote these Twelve Steps are probably unaware of their origin, it is a shame that these steps have been introduced into the church with such fanfare.

An Inside Look

What goes on at an AA meeting? A number of years ago a recovering alcoholic invited me to attend an open AA meeting (some meetings are closed to the public). The woman who gave the invitation was a chain smoker, and when I arrived at the meeting, I discovered that a number of the other recovering alcoholics in attendance were also smokers. The room was saturated with smoke and swearing was freely heard. Each individual introduced himself or herself with the phrase: "My name is _____, and I am an alcoholic." (Only first names are supposed to be used in AA.) Oh, sure, the "Serenity Prayer" was read at the beginning of the meeting, and they mentioned a "Higher Power," but this "Higher Power" was unable to deliver them from a number of other sins besides alcoholism. These people may have been sober, but the only difference between them and those who are still alcoholics is that the alcoholic is an intoxicated sinner and the AA individual is a sober sinner. Many will claim to be a Christian, but their lives do not bear fruit of this testimony. A Christian is a person who follows Christ and obeys His commands. One Biblical command is: "As He which hath called you is holy, so BE YE HOLY in ALL manner of conversation" (I Peter 1:15). The Greek word for "conversation" takes in more than just a person's speech. It originally included a person's entire mode of life, character, and behavior. So, when the Bible mentions that we are to be holy in our conversation it means that all of our actions are also to be holy and in accordance with God's Word.

Did the co-founders of Alcoholics Anonymous have holy lives after they founded AA? You can decide for yourself with the following information. One book written by a recovering alcoholic, Nan Robertson, who highly endorses AA, states this about Dr. Bob Smith: "He relished a dirty joke...."[15] She also mentions about Bill Wilson's lifestyle:

> ...particularly during his sober decades in A.A. in the forties, fifties and sixties, Bill Wilson was a **COMPULSIVE WOMANIZER.** His flirtations and his **ADULTEROUS** behavior filled him with guilt, according to old-timers close to him, but he continued to stray off the reservation. His last and most serious love affair, with a woman at A.A. headquarters in New York, began when he was in his sixties. She was important to him until the end of his life, and was remembered in a financial agreement with A.A. This affair, and experiments in **SPIRITUALISM,** LSD and megavitamin therapy, scandalized A.A. trustees and other veterans in the home office....

His most controversial searches revolved around SEANCES and the hallucinogen LSD....

In the last twenty years of Bill's life, he shocked A.A. trustees and old-timers not only by TAKING LOVERS but with his experiments with LSD, his crusades for niacin to solve mental problems and the SPIRITUALISTIC SEANCES he organized at Stepping Stones [the name he gave to his residence]. [Emphasis added.][16]

Later in this book we are told that Bill was also a "heavy, sloppy smoker all his life...."[17] Additionally, several of the books that were APPROVED by the AA board contain a good dose of cursing.

AA Endorses False Gods

It is true that AA's environment is not conducive to Christian living and guidance, but is it a fair assessment to say that AA's "Higher Power" could be a false god or even SATAN? Are counterfeit gods acceptable to AA? They may say that a "Higher Power" is the AA group, but certainly they wouldn't believe that the "Higher Power" would be a false god, would they? Are others gods like Allah, Buddha, Tao, Shiva, Lucifer, Kali, or ANY other "God" acceptable in AA beliefs? Turning again to APPROVED literature from AA, we find our answer:

Much to our relief, we discovered that we did not need to consider another's conception of God. Our own conception, however inadequate, was sufficient to make the approach and to effect a contact with Him. As soon as we admitted the possible existence of a Creative Intelligence, a Spirit of the Universe underlying the totality of things, we began to be possessed of a new sense of power and direction, provided we took other simple steps. We found that God does not make too hard terms with those who seek Him. To us, THE REALM OF SPIRIT IS BROAD, ROOMY, ALL INCLUSIVE; NEVER EXCLUSIVE OR FORBIDDING to those who earnestly seek. It is open, we believe, to all men.

> When, therefore, we speak to you of God, WE MEAN YOUR OWN CONCEPTION OF GOD. [Emphasis added.][18]

Obviously, "your own conception of God" can mean ANY false god. Sirhan Sirhan, assassin of U.S. Senator Robert Kennedy, is supposed to be leading an Alcoholics Anonymous group in the Soledad prison. Clearly Sirhan Sirhan's "Higher Power" cannot be the God of the Bible since he was a Moslem and also a Rosicrucian.[19] The Rosicrucian Order (AMORC), by the way, is an esoteric occult group. Another supporter of AA is Sharon Gless, a TV actress, who credits her success to the demonic spirit guide, Lazaris.[20] Again, it should be unmistakable that AA's "Higher Power" is definitely not the God of the Bible, but AA literature makes it even plainer that other gods are acceptable. One particular alcoholic couldn't accept the idea of a "Higher Power." This is his account of how his AA sponsor explained it to him:

> THEN HE ASKS ME IF I BELIEVE IN A POWER GREATER THAN MYSELF, WHETHER I CALL THAT POWER GOD, *ALLAH, CONFUCIUS*, PRIME CAUSE, DIVINE MIND, OR *ANY OTHER NAME*. I told him that I believe in electricity and other forces of nature, but as for a God, if there is one, He has never done anything for me....
>
> "Then all of your troubles are over," says the man and leaves the room. [Emphasis added.][21]

One more example should suffice. One day a letter from a Presbyterian minister arrived at the AA headquarters. The minister wrote the following:

> We took A.A.'s Twelve Steps over to the largest **BUDDHIST** monastery in this province. We showed them to the priest at the head of it. After he had finished looking over the Twelve Steps, the monk said, "Why, these are fine! Since we as Buddhists don't understand God just as you do, it might be slightly more acceptable if you inserted the word 'good' in your Steps instead of 'God.' Nevertheless, you say in these Steps that it is God *as*

you understand Him. That clears up the point for us. Yes, A.A.'s **TWELVE STEPS WILL CERTAINLY BE ACCEPTED BY THE BUDDHISTS** around here." [Italics in the original; Bold and capitals added.][22]

Maybe professing Christians do not fully understand the implications of a "God as you understand Him," but the Buddhists sure do!

The Unknown God

The Bible does not teach some vague, wishy-washy, nebulous concept of God. On one occasion the apostle Paul was in Athens and noticed that the city was full of idolatry and superstition (Acts 17:16). As he passed through the city he observed that an altar had been erected and this inscription was on it: "TO THE UNKNOWN GOD." It is interesting to note that the Greek word for "unknown" is "agnostos" or "NOT KNOWING." Many people who enter Alcoholics Anonymous claim that they are "agnostics," ones who DO NOT KNOW if there is a God. In this sense, the Athenians and numerous AAs have something in common.

The Athenian "god" could well be described as a "God as YOU understand Him." This "god" could fit anybody's perception, but we are not to make up our own concept of God. A god created in our own image is a MAN-MADE god. This kind of a god will never save you and is a god LIMITED by your imagination. A god like this was not adequate, so Paul told these people: "Whom therefore ye ignorantly worship, Him declare I unto you" (Acts 17:23). It was not good enough for these people to worship or believe in a god as THEY understood or comprehended Him. The Athenians, like those in AA, were religious and had a yearning to worship *something* or *someone,* but an undefined and unknowable God cannot answer prayers. Hebrews 11:6 reveals that "without faith it is impossible to please Him [God]; for he that cometh to God must believe that HE IS, and that He is a rewarder of them that DILIGENTLY seek Him." This certainly is different than what is taught in AA. AA tells the newcomer that he doesn't have to believe in a PERSONAL God. Even the AA group would suffice, but the Bible clearly states that for a person to come to God he must believe that GOD IS. The God of the Bible, Paul explained, had specific qualities and was not a nameless entity. Paul described this God to the Athenians as the One Who:

> ... made the world and all things therein, seeing that He is Lord of heaven and earth, [and] dwelleth not in temples made with hands; Neither is worshipped with men's hands, as though He needed any thing, seeing He giveth to all life, and breath, and all things....we ought not to think that the Godhead is like unto gold, or silver, or stone, graven by art and man's device. And the times of this ignorance God winked at; but NOW commandeth all men every where to repent... (Acts 17:24-25, 29-30).

The AA notion of a "God as YOU understand Him" cannot be accurately described as the same God who is clearly revealed in the Bible.

5. AA IS RELIGIOUS!

Is AA religious? Since AA denies being religious, let's decide for ourselves if they are religious or not by looking at some statements from a variety of AA sources:

1. The A.A. program of recovery from alcoholism is UNDENIABLY BASED ON ACCEPTANCE OF CERTAIN SPIRITUAL VALUES. The individual member is free to interpret those values as he or she thinks best, or not to think about them at all. [Emphasis added.][1]

2. The fact is that the SPIRITUAL perception of most members deepens the longer they are in A.A. and try to follow the Twelve Steps. [Emphasis added.][2]

3. As soon as a man can say that he does believe, or is willing to believe, we emphatically assure him that he is on his way. It has been repeatedly proven among us that upon this simple cornerstone a wonderfully effective SPIRITUAL structure can be built.... [Emphasis added.][3]

4. [One Indian A.A. member said:] "To me, program is SPIRITUAL. I feel Great Spirit at all meetings and when talk to A.A. friends. I know peace." [Emphasis added.][4]

5. The society of Alcoholics Anonymous is SPIRITUALLY as well as morally centered. Nearly every A.A. member comes to believe in and depend upon a higher Power which most of us call God. In A.A. practically no full recovery from alcoholism has been possible without this all-important FAITH. God, *as we understand Him,* is the foundation upon which our fellowship rests. [Italics in the original; Bold and capitals added.][5]

6. [One testimonial statement says:] "I read the book and God leapt at me from every page."[6]

7. Do not let any prejudice you may have against SPIRITUAL terms deter you from honestly asking yourself what they mean to you. At the start, this was all we needed to commence SPIRITUAL growth, to effect our first conscious relation with God as we understood Him. [Emphasis added.][7]

8. Never talk down to an alcoholic from any moral or spiritual hilltop; simply LAY OUT THE KIT OF SPIRITUAL TOOLS for his inspection. [Emphasis added.][8]

9. So we of A.A. do obey SPIRITUAL principles. [Emphasis added.][9]

10. The material payoff, as well as the SPIRITUAL payoff, of A.A.'s way of life is downright incredible. [Emphasis added.][10]

11. A.A. can and will survive so long as it remains a SPIRITUAL FAITH and a way of life open to all men and women who suffer from alcoholism. [Emphasis added.][11]

12. God was certainly there in our Steps, but He was now expressed in terms that anybody—*anybody at all*—could accept and try. [Emphasis in the original.][12]

13. It is through Sam Shoemaker that most of A.A.'s SPIRITUAL principles have come.[13]

14. The terms "SPIRITUAL EXPERIENCE" and "SPIRITUAL AWAKENING" are used MANY TIMES in this book.... [Emphasis added.][14]

Religious But Not Religious

I could list scores (perhaps hundreds) of other such references to RELIGIOUS terminology. After all the mention in AA literature of a "spiritual awakening," "God," a "Higher Power," and "prayer," doesn't it seem like AA is a religion or at least religious in nature? The simple fact is that AA repudiates this! Just ONE PARAGRAPH before stating that the "A.A. program of recovery from alcoholism is UNDENIABLY based on acceptance of certain SPIRITUAL values," is this comment: "A.A. is not a religious society, since it requires no definite religious belief as a condition of membership."[15]

Regardless of this denial, AA IS religious. Reading through numerous pamphlets and books which are approved by AA, shows definitely that AA is religious in nature. Since AA is not Christianity, yet it promotes a spirituality, what kind of spirituality is represented? Although many individuals in AA are unaware of it, Alcoholics Anonymous actually is encouraging New Age beliefs and practices. For example, let's look at the meaning of the "SPIRITUAL AWAKENING" frequently mentioned in AA's books. We are told that practicing the Twelve Steps laid down by AA brings about "a SPIRITUAL AWAKENING."[16] Wanda Marrs explains:

> The word *awakening* is a popular one among New Age teachers. As his spirit guides told Ken Carey, "your race is soon to experience widespread *awakenings*, or as some will see it, a massive descent of beings from the stars."

> It is no mistake, then, that Alcoholics Anonymous and other twelve step programs as well as the practicers of tantric sex, uniformly speak of an *awakening* that occurs. That awakening is, in effect, the acceptance of the Goddess into the human being. An awakening happens when a person is *possessed* by the Goddess. Or, better stated, a person is possessed by *demons* who slavishly endeavor to remold the individual into the Goddess image desired by their master, Satan. [Emphasis in the original.][17]

New Age Ties

There are other connections to the New Age as well. Coleman Publishing bills itself as "rapidly becoming this nation's leading book, audio and video publishing company in the Spiritual, Self Help and NEW AGE field." [Emphasis added.][18] One author that is promoted is David R. Hawkins, M.D., a psychiatrist and director of the Institute of Spiritual Research in Sedona, Arizona. Hawkins has been working in the field of alcoholism and in "the late 60s he worked with Bill

Wilson, founder of AA on the relationship between nutrition and alcoholism and together with Bill wrote Bills (sic) Communication to AA's Physicians."[19] Since 1965, Hawkins has been a member of the First Zen Institute of New York. Zen is one form of Buddhism, a pagan religion.

The *New Age Journal* has a section entitled "Directory of New Age Resources." One of the "New Age" organizations mentioned is the National Council on Alcoholism (now known as the National Council on Alcoholism and Drug Dependence) in New York. I have received some pamphlets and other literature from this group. One of these brochures recommends the meetings and programs of Al-Anon, Alateen, and Adult Children of Alcoholics (ACOA or ACA) for family members of alcoholics, as well as mentioning that information on alcoholism can be obtained from AA.[20] Their endorsement of AA goes even further. In their 1989 Annual Report, they mention that a television production about AA's co-founder entitled "My Name is Bill W.," lists the National Council on Alcoholism and Drug Dependence's (NCADD) toll-free number.[21] Also, the 27th Conference held by NCADD was dedicated to Lois Burnham Wilson, the co-founder of the Al-Anon Family Groups and wife of Bill Wilson. Mrs. Wilson was a "friend of NCADD founder Marty Mann."[22] Marty Mann, by the way, was the first woman to achieve sobriety through Alcoholics Anonymous, joining AA in 1939. We are told that she was "one of the most celebrated and loved women in A.A.'s history."[23]

World Goodwill, a well-known New Age organization, listed some groups that participated in their World Service Forum in the past. Some of the more familiar groups are: Planetary Citizens, World Future Society, Greenpeace, Amnesty International, UNESCO, Oxfam America, Psychosynthesis Institute of New York, The Theosophical Society, Brahma Kumaris World Spiritual University, and the United Nations Development Fund for Women, among others. **ALL** of these groups just mentioned, **WITHOUT EXCEPTION**, are New Age organizations in practice and philosophy. Among this listing can also be found "Alcoholics Anonymous!"[24] Furthermore, the World Service Forum offers cassettes from some past speakers at their Forums. One of the guest lecturers was "Bill of Alcoholics Anonymous."[25] What does this say about AA?

AA's Logo

Even AA's logo is interesting. It is a circle enclosing a triangle. Both of these symbols are important and popular in the New Age. Bill Wilson tells us that the "circle stands for the whole world of A.A., and the triangle stands for A.A.'s Three Legacies of Recovery, Unity, and Service."[26] That explanation doesn't seem too bad, but then Wilson adds:

> That we have chosen this particular symbol is perhaps no accident. The priests and seers of antiquity regarded the circle enclosing the triangle as a means of warding off spirits of evil, and A.A.'s circle and triangle of Recovery, Unity, and Service has certainly meant all of that to us and much more.[27]

It is quite indisputable that he knew what the symbol meant. Of course, it should come as no great amazement since he was already involved in seances and spiritualism.

Yet another linkage to the New Age can be found in the *Addiction and Consciousness Journal*. A treatment program for alcoholics and addicts includes "education as to the nature of addiction and further enquiry into the nature of spiritual experience in the recovery process."[28] Notice what type of education is presented: "Spiritual disciplines such as the TWELVE STEPS, *A Course in Miracles*, Hatha Yoga, and other SPIRITUAL programs will be incorporated." [Emphasis added.][29] Hatha Yoga is an exercise that is based on the occultic Hindu religion. *A Course in Miracles* is a study course which is used as a New Age "Bible." This book was received through demonic intervention via automatic writing.

In 1965, psychologist Helen Cohn Schucman, employed at the Psychiatry Department of New York's Columbia University College of Physicians and Surgeons, began to vaguely sense and then clearly hear an inner voice. A trained psychologist as well as an atheist and a disbeliever in the paranormal, she didn't know what to make of it. She told a colleague, "You know that inner voice? It won't leave me alone! It keeps saying, 'This is a course in miracles. Please take notes.' What am I supposed to do?" The colleague responded, "Why don't you take notes? Take them down in that shorthand you use." "But what if it's gibberish?" Helen responded. "Then I'll *know* I'm crazy."

In her first clairaudient dictation session, Helen claimed to receive and record what was later to become the first introductory page of the *Text*, the first of three volumes [called *A Course in Miracles*.] [Emphasis in the original.][30]

Among these New Age and occult practices are listed the Twelve Step programs! As mentioned earlier, the Twelve Step programs originated with Alcoholics Anonymous through the influence of the Oxford Group. Notice also that all of these techniques are listed as "SPIRITUAL disciplines." Yes, AA is religious, but it is not based on Christianity—it is based on occultic methods. Therefore, it is no great surprise to see New Agers endorsing AA and its Twelve Steps. What is astonishing is that Christian leaders are promoting AA.

AA and the Occult Connection

Marilyn Ferguson, a prominent and well-known New Ager, also gives her endorsement of Alcoholics Anonymous. In listing ways in which a person could ALTER CONSCIOUSNESS, she included the following items: Biofeedback, sensory isolation, hypnosis, meditation, Zen, yoga, est, Lifespring, Silva Mind Control, dervish dancing, shamanistic rituals, fantasy games (Dungeons and Dragons, etc.), dreams, Jungian analysis, primal therapy, Gestalt, rebirthing, martial arts (T'ai Chi Ch'uan, karate, aikido), rolfing, bioenergetics, and applied kinesiology.[31] Would you believe that among all these occult subjects, self-help groups such as AA were recommended as well?[32]

> Concerning these kinds of experiences, Ferguson comments: "**ALL** of these approaches might be called *psychotechnologies*— systems for a **DELIBERATE CHANGE IN CONSCIOUS-NESS.**" [Italics in the original; Bold and capitals added.][33]

One more factor that should cause concern is a comparison made by Ed Dowling, a Jesuit priest who spoke at AA's twentieth anniversary. Bill Wilson said that it was Dowling who "had been the first to note how closely in principle A.A.'s Twelve Steps paralleled a part of the Exercises of St. Ignatius, a basic spiritual discipline of the Jesuit order.[34] St. Ignatius of Loyola was the founder of the Society of Jesus, which is better known as the Jesuits.[35] These exercises were practiced with the help of a "director." "Beside sight, the other senses such as hearing, smell, taste and touch will play their part. In short, it is mere controlled auto-suggestion."[36]

Not only should the description of these exercises remind us of the occult practice of visualization, but it should also bring to remembrance the "house parties" and "quiet times" of the Oxford Group. No wonder Dowling recognized the similarities! I just wish Christians could be as perceptive as Dowling was.

The Broad Highway

Actually, AA's own statements should let us know where they are coming from. For example, they brag:

> Such were the final concessions to those of little or no faith; this was the great contribution of our atheists and agnostics. They had **WIDENED OUR GATEWAY** so that ALL who suffer might pass through, regardless of their belief or *lack of belief*.

> God was certainly there in our Steps, but He was NOW expressed in terms that anybody—*anybody at all*—could accept

and try. Countless A.A.'s have since testified that without this great evidence of LIBERALITY they never could have set foot on any path of spiritual progress or even approached us in the first place. [Italics in the original; Bold and capitals added.][37]

Another AA book gives them away even moreso:

We can only clear the ground a bit. If our testimony helps sweep away prejudice, enables you to think honestly, encourages you to search diligently within yourself, then, if you wish, YOU CAN JOIN US ON THE BROAD HIGHWAY. With this attitude you cannot fail.[38]

What is wrong with joining them on the BROAD HIGHWAY? The Bible answers this question with these words:

Enter ye in at the strait gate: for WIDE IS THE GATE, and BROAD IS THE WAY, that leadeth to DESTRUCTION, and MANY there be which go in thereat: Because strait is the gate, and narrow is the way, which leadeth unto life, and few there be that find it. BEWARE OF FALSE PROPHETS, which come to you in sheep's clothing, but inwardly they are ravening wolves. Ye shall know them by their fruits (Matthew 7:13-16).

We have already seen the fruit that the founders of AA have produced—adultery, smoking, dirty jokes, LSD, seances, and spiritualism. Yes, we can know them by their fruits and we can also know that the BROAD HIGHWAY that AA brags about will only lead to DESTRUCTION.

6. AA'S GODPARENT: CARL JUNG

Recognizing the closeness of some New Age ties with the AA may fall more into place if we look at Carl Jung, another important influence on AA's spirituality. One catalog advertising a small book entitled *AA'S Godparents: Three Early Influences on Alcoholics Anonymous* by Igor I. Sikorsky, Jr. says this:

> This fascinating readable book explores the early days of AA and the influence of three nonalcoholics—psychiatrist Carl Jung, theologian Emmet Fox, and writer Jack Alexander—on its founding philosophy, spiritual direction, and growth.[1]

Out of these three individuals, we are going to focus in on Carl Jung.

Swiss psychologist and psychiatrist Carl Gustav Jung (July 26, 1875-June 6, 1961) was born in Basel. He was the founder of analytic psychology and studied under Pierre Janet. In 1907 Jung met Freud for the first time and became his foremost disciple. He continued his association with Freud until 1912 when he formulated his own theories, especially the idea of the collective unconscious,[2] which is very popular in the New Age movement today.

Jung's introduction to the world of the occult came at a very early age.

> ... Jung had been deeply involved in occultism since childhood, as had his parents, grandparents, and other relatives before him. The home in which his mother was raised was so infested with "ghosts" that as a girl she had to hold the "spirits" at bay long enough for her father (who was himself a medium as well as a Protestant minister) to write out his Sunday sermon. "Every week, at a fixed hour, he used to hold intimate conversations with his deceased first wife, very much to the chagrin of the second," who "could also see 'spirits.'"[3]

The New Age journal, *New Times*, states that

> Carl Jung studied paranormal events early in his career and continued to be fascinated by them throughout his life. His research into Western Mystery traditions—especially alchemy—has made him a favorite of occultists....[4]

He even "regarded alchemy as the predecessor of modern *psychology*." [Emphasis added.][5]

One New Age newsletter lists Jung in a "Who's Who in Meditation" as one of several people who had obtained personal charisma through "yoga-like meditation."[6] *The American Theosophist*, a magazine put out by the occult Theosophical Society, tells us that "Jung's psychology is seen to be more in line with yoga."[7]

Jung and Reincarnation

A belief in reincarnation was held by Jung. He commented: "I can well imagine that I might have lived in former centuries... that I had to be born again because I had not fulfilled the task given to me."[8]

Marilyn Ferguson, the New Age author of *The Aquarian Conspiracy*, listed Jung as one of "the four most frequently mentioned individuals who have influenced New Agers."[9] Nat Freedland informs us that it was Jung

> ... who did more than any other twentieth-century thinker to make occult theorizing respectable. Profound Jungian interpretations seem to emerge everywhere in a serious study of contemporary OCCULT philosophy....
>
> Much of Jung's deepest OCCULT thinking went into his extremely ambitious prefaces for the first Western translations of the *I Ching*, China's ancient method of divining psychic trends and directions integral to a present situation; *The Secret of the Golden Flower*, the Chinese Taoist method of meditation; and the *Tibetan Book of the Dead*, which he saw as using reincarnation to symbolize "an initiation process whose purpose

it is to restore to the soul the divinity it lost at birth." [Emphasis added.][10]

Speaking about the "divinity" that mankind supposedly lost at birth is another popular theme that has been espoused and promoted in New Age circles. This refers to the idea that humans are God and takes us all the way back in history to the Garden of Eden where Satan told Eve that she would be as God (Genesis 3:1-7). This idea has permeated the occult, New Age, and metaphysical communities. Sadly, many of our churches have also fallen for this lie of Satan. Notice also that AA can fit into this category of believing that humankind is God. If you remember, their statements that the AA group can serve as the alcoholic's "Higher Power" certainly qualify them as supporting this theory. Additionally, AA teaches that ANYONE or ANYTHING can be God, and that definitely includes human beings, so the AA does accept the godhood of individuals as a possibility.

Jung also wrote a foreword to New Ager Suzuki's book entitled *Introduction to Zen Buddhism*.[11] Also, the *I Ching*, which Jung endorsed, is another occultic sensation. Jung, who "was an avid devotee of the *I Ching*,"[12] even wrote a preface to the Wilhelm-Baynes Translation of this book, but before he did so, he first consulted the *I Ching*.[13] The *I Ching* or *Book of Changes* is a method of divination, a means of foretelling the future. The Bible explicitly forbids us to practice divination (see Deuteronomy 18:10-12; II Kings 17:17-18, etc.).

Jung's family history was rooted in occultic practices,[14] including Freemasonry[15] (his grandfather was head of the Swiss Freemasons). Carl Jung was also a pro-Nazi supporter.[16] We are told:

> Jung himself grew up in an atmosphere of seances and persistent poltergeist activity. He had his first psychic vision at the age of three. And at an even earlier age than [psychologist Carl] Rogers, he too renounced the austere and formal Protestant

Christianity in which he was raised. The occult, however, was an obsession which Jung could never escape.... In a series of lectures in 1897 to a student organization at Basel University while an undergraduate there, the 22-year-old Jung said that "the soul does exist, it is intelligent and immortal, not subject to time and space." He also affirmed "the reality of spirits and spiritualism, on the evidence of telekinesis, messages of dying people, hypnotism, clairvoyance... and prophetic dreams."[17]

Jung Scares Freud

In fact, Jung intentionally caused poltergeist activity to occur on two different occasions while in Freud's presence, which scared Freud tremendously.[18] Occultism was so much a part of his life that he was called the "Hexenmeister"[19] or "The Warlock of Zurich."[20] Jung, like many New Agers today, also believed in a guiding figure (a spirit guide) that he referred to as a "wise old man."[21] He explained the "wise old man" like this:

> The figure of the wise old man can appear so plastically, not only in dreams but also in visionary meditation (or what we call "active imagination"), that, as is sometimes apparently the case in India, it takes over the role of a guru. The wise old man appears in dreams in the guise of a magician, doctor, priest, teacher, professor, grandfather, or any other person possessing authority. The archetype of spirit in the shape of a man, hobgoblin, or animal always appears in a situation where insight, understanding, good advice, determination, planning, etc., are needed but cannot be mustered on one's own resources. The archetype compensates this state of spiritual deficiency by contents designed to fill in the gap.[22]

Jung's belief in spirit guides was a reality for him, for he had several of his own personal guides, one of which was named Philemon.[23] "He painted the image of Philemon on the second-story bedroom wall of his Tower at Bollingen, so intimately did he feel the influence of this marginal guide in his daily life."[24] Philemon

... appeared to Jung as a wise old man "with a long white beard, the horns of a bull, and the wings of a kingfisher," [and] gave him all kinds of insights concerning the "collective unconscious" and other mysteries....[25]

One of Jung's books, *Seven Sermons to the Dead,* "appears to have been written through automatic writing during a period when the Jung family was undergoing a large number of occultic events in their home."[26] Jon Klimo, writing in the *New Age Journal,* stated that Jung reported "a number of personal experiences that resembled channeling."[27] It is recounted that "Jung constantly felt an ominous presence about him and the Jung children reportedly saw 'ghostly entities in the house.'"[28] In addition, Jung practiced necromancy,[29] which is divination by communicating with the dead.

The Bible specifically warns us:

> There shall not be found among you any one that maketh his son or his daughter to pass through the fire, or that useth DIVINATION, or an observer of times, or an enchanter, or a witch. Or a charmer, or a CONSULTER WITH FAMILIAR SPIRITS [spirit guides], or a wizard, or a NECROMANCER. For ALL that do these things are an abomination unto the Lord... (Deuteronomy 18:10-12).

Jung himself must have known that the spirit guides were not of a godly source, for at one point he stated: "But there was a demonic strength in me."[30] "I had great difficulty to control my thoughts. There was a demon in me...."[31]

Use of Horoscopes

> At his Zurich clinic [Jung] had horoscopes charted for every new patient. He said he found the charts useful as a preliminary diagram of the forces operating within a patient's total personality.[32]

The word "horoscope" comes from the Greek word "horoskopos" which means "one who observes the hour." Horoscopes are drawn up by astrologers or those who study the sun, moon, stars, and planets to foretell future events. The astrologers claim that the position of these heavenly bodies at the exact time of one's birth will influence this person's entire life including his personality, romance, and career. Given the exact time and location of one's birth, astrologers allege that they can then determine which days will be "lucky" and which days will be "bad." These good and bad days differ from person to person. If March 25th has been determined as a good day for you, you would then be encouraged to make a large business deal, apply for that special job opening that you've always wanted, or take that long-awaited trip to Europe on THAT day. However, if March 25th is one of your bad days, you should not make any major decision until one of your "good" days, thus avoiding the possibility of having things turn sour. "[A]strology is clearly the **MOST IMPORTANT** part of the **OCCULT** explosion." [Emphasis added.][33]

Not only is astrology a pseudoscience, there are many conflicting ideas and horoscope readings among astrologers themselves.[34] In addition to the inconsistencies and contradictions of astrology and the astrologers, there are also Biblical warnings that no one should be involved in such practices because they are clearly not of God (see Deuteronomy 18:10-12; Jeremiah 10:2; Isaiah 47:10-15; II Kings 17:16-18, etc.) There are several reasons why God WILL NOT ALLOW His children to dabble with astrology. One reason is that the stars were originally viewed as deities, or gods,[35] thus causing the individual to worship the creation more than the Creator which Romans 1 condemns. Also, people who depend on the horoscope feel that they are not accountable to God for their actions. After all, if man's destiny lies in the stars, then whatever he does has already been determined. He really did not make his own decision, so how could he be held accountable for something that he had no part in deciding? Thus, the horoscope becomes an alibi for a sinful life. Astrology (including horoscopes and other forms of divination) is, and ALWAYS HAS BEEN, associated with the OCCULT and WITCHCRAFT.

Jung's Influence on AA

We have just touched the surface of Jung and some of his occultic practices, but what does this have to do with his influence on Alcoholics Anonymous? The connection is this: A friend of Ebby's, who was the friend of Alcoholics Anonymous's co-founder, Bill Wilson, was also a drunk. He had gone to Dr. Jung for psychotherapy and felt that he had acquired enough knowledge to conquer his alcoholism, but in a short time he was drunk again. Returning to Jung, he begged him to tell him why he had not been able to control his drinking and Jung said that he was utterly hopeless. In despair, this man questioned the Dr. further and asked if there were ever any exceptions. Jung replied that what was needed would be a "spiritual experience."[36]

> Puzzled but intrigued, the man then went in search of a spiritual awakening. When he found it, he passed it on to Bill Wilson and his associates, who had already been influenced by the spirituality of the charismatic Oxford Group in England. In response to these influences, Wilson and his associates developed what we now know as the 12 Step recovery program for alcoholics.[37]

Actually, a closer look at Jung and the Oxford Group brings out many striking similarities between the two. Consider, for instance, Jung's involvement with occultic activities. Frank Buchman, like Jung, advocated the occultic practice of automatic writing. In fact, one of Buchman's close disciples was Arthur James (A. J.) Russell. It was Russell who wrote *For Sinners Only,* which is considered to be one of the most popular "scriptures" for the Buchmanites.[38] It is no wonder that this book was important to the Oxford Group (the "Buchmanites") because in it Russell endorsed Buchman as a spiritual giant.[39] It is reported in *For Sinners Only* that spirit beings which could not be identified by Russell gave him information about where to get his writings published, so we can see that both the Oxford Groups and Jung had spirit (actually demonic) guidance with some of their writings.

Which God Is Calling?

Another book, *God Calling,* lists Russell as its editor. This book was produced by two anonymous women who received the information during their Quiet Times. If you remember, during this Quiet Time the Oxford Groupers "would lie on their beds or sit in silent groups, with pencil and paper."[40] As thoughts came to them, notes would be made. It was during these sessions of automatic writing, that the book *God Calling* came to be.[41] Although it is claimed that the book was written by "God," we know that this cannot be true for God condemns occultic practices (which automatic writing is). Therefore, He would not use a forbidden procedure through which to convey His message. Also, God does not contradict Himself and this book is filled with information that directly contradicts God's Word, the Bible. One instance would be where this book "recommends that readers *contact and keep company with spirits in the unseen world* (see Sept. 6th devotional in *God Calling*)."[42]

Sadly, so-called Christian publishers have printed this book and many "Christian" bookstores are selling it. In fact, *God Calling* has been on the best-selling list of Christian books for a number of years.[43] Yet another indication that this book IS NOT a Christian book is that it is sold by the esoteric Theosophical Society.[44] This organization promotes reincarnation, channeling, yoga, evolution, and numerous other occultic theories and practices, so it would seem probable that if they are selling *God Calling,* it most likely falls into at least one of the endorsed OCCULT categories for their books.

Seances and LSD

Seances and spiritualism were part of Jung's life; they were also ingredients that helped to make up Bill Wilson's life. At Bill's residence, which he called Stepping Stones, seances were held. For decades of Bill's life after he sobered up, he engaged in searching for answers through spiritualism, not to mention experimenting with hallucinatory drugs like LSD.[45]

Jung rejected Christianity.[46] Although the Oxford Group and Alcoholics Anonymous may not have officially denounced Christianity, they certainly do not believe that one must be a Christian to receive the benefits of the group. AA's co-founder, Bill Wilson, stated his view of Christianity and Christ like this:

> With ministers, and the world's religions, I parted right there. When they talked of a God personal to me, who was love, superhuman strength and direction, I became irritated and my mind snapped shut against such a theory.

> To Christ I conceded that certainty of a great man, not too closely followed by those who claimed Him. His moral teaching—most excellent. For myself, **I HAD ADOPTED THOSE PARTS WHICH SEEMED CONVENIENT AND NOT TOO DIFFICULT; THE REST I DISCARDED....**

> Despite the living example of my friend [Ebby] there remained in me the vestiges of my old prejudice. **THE WORD GOD STILL AROUSED A CERTAIN ANTIPATHY.** When the thought was expressed that there might be a God personal to me this feeling was intensified. I didn't like the idea. I could go for such conceptions as Creative Intelligence, Universal Mind or Spirit of Nature but I resisted the thought of a Czar of the Heavens, however loving His sway might be. [Emphasis added.][47]

Ebby, realizing that Bill wasn't ready to accept the Biblical view of God, made a suggestion: "Why don't you choose your own conception of God?"[48] Bill loved this view. He writes:

*It was only a matter of being willing to believe in a Power
greater than myself. Nothing more was required of me to make
my beginning.* I saw that growth could start from that point. Upon
a foundation of complete willingness I might build what I saw in
my friend. Would I have it? Of course I would! [Emphasis in the
original.][49]

Collective Consciousness

Bill was willing to believe in a "Creative Intelligence, Universal
Mind or Spirit of Nature"[50] but he could not acknowledge a personal
God. Likewise, Jung held to a belief in a Universal Mind which he
called the "collective consciousness."[51] The collective consciousness
is the central tenet in Jungian psychology.

… Jung theorized that there was a deeper level of unconscious
content beneath the Freudian personal unconscious. Within this
"deep mind" were the memories of the race: its cultural, religious,
spiritual, mythological development. Religion for Jung was
innate, inbred. He defined the collective unconscious as
impersonal and transpersonal, transcending one's own personal
experience.

According to the Jungian theory, we are not merely connected
to our own personal experiences of the past, but as members of
the human race we are also connected to the collective
Unconscious of mankind and thereby receive a psychic inheritance
containing in latent fashion all that has gone on before.[52]

An ad for "Ritual Magic" tapes by Dick Sutphen, a New Ager,
tells us that through the use of magic, rituals, and invocations, you can
"tap into a very real channel of vibrational energy in the collective
consciousness that exists externally as the creation of all who came
before you and used this power."[53] The ad continues:

For his *Ritual Magic* tapes, Dick draws upon his extensive
background in the occult and eclectic, esoteric sources including
the mystical *Qabalah*, and the *Key of Solomon*—the infamous

magical textbook which exists in various manuscripts in the British Museum, and dates back to first century A.D.[54]

Jung's collective consciousness is called the "noosphere" by Teilhard de Chardin, "psi bank" by Jose Arguelles, and the "Akashic Records" by spiritualists[55] and Hindus.[56] Anyone even slightly familiar with the occult should recognize this last term for the Akashic Records have been a "longtime mainstay of occultism and magic."[57] Maharishi Mahesh Yogi, the founder of the occult technique of Transcendental Meditation (TM), as well as numerous New Agers and occultists, write of these records.[58] In fact, one occultist, Richard Kieninger (aka Eklal Kueshana), tells us that the Akashic Records play an important role in the theories of reincarnation and karma.[59] Edgar Cayce, a psychic and trance medium, was supposedly "psychically attuned to the Akashic Records."[60] It is claimed that a good psychic can plug into the vibrations in the Akashic Records and see the past, thereby being able to "tell you what your previous lives were like."[61]

AA Not Based on Christianity

It is clear to see that both AA and the Oxford Groups were not (and still are not) based on Christianity. In fact, Roy Livesey had attended one Moral Rearmament (Oxford Group) conference where speakers and participants represented different world religions, but the message of this conference was that "no one should 'fall into the trap and seek only one God.'"[62]

> Buchman's Oxford Group was not exclusively Christian. One could be a Hindu, a Moslem, or a Buddhist and be a member. Indeed, Buchman is known to have traveled to India where it is believed he conspired with Hindu initiates of The Order and worked to set up chapters of the Oxford Group.[63]

Eastern religion, especially Zen Buddhism, appealed to Jung.[64] Likewise, Buchman catered to the Buddhists and other religions when trying to organize a Moral Rearmament group in other countries.

... MRA [Moral Rearmament or the Oxford Group] must, therefore, be so projected in India that it would not seem to the most devout Hindu or Moslem to be just another Christian mission. So we find that in MRA propaganda designed for the oriental market there is practically no mention of Christianity: Christ, **IF NAMED AT ALL**, is sandwiched unobtrusively between Gautama the Buddha and Mahatma Gandhi; the suggestion is that, whatever your faith, you will be the better—a better Hindu or Buddhist or Moslem—for accepting MRA's rule of life; and **THIS RULE OF LIFE**, so far as it is theistic at all, **IS CONSISTENT... WITH** a relatively undogmatic **PANTHEISM**. [Emphasis added.][65]

Buchman had even attracted the attention and respect of the Buddhist community. Below is described a ritual that took place in the late 1950's:

The colorful assembly rose in standing ovation in the high-raftered hall as the Lord Abbot of Watmahadtat monastery, who is also Minister of the Interior for Ecclesiastical Affairs in Thailand, in his saffron robes presented a ceremonial gong to Dr (sic) Buchman. He struck the gong four times, saying that each powerfully ringing note symbolised one of the absolute standards of MRA.... It was the first time that such a high official of the Buddhist hierarchy had left Asia...

As a token of the response of the Buddhist world to Buchman's leadership, the Lord Abbot presented him with a gold medal bearing the image of the Emerald Buddha.[66]

Buchman also

... saw no inconsistency in saying that MRA had "the answer... that unites the Moslem with all men who truly live their faith" and that the Moslem nations could be "a girder of unity for the whole world," **WHILE HE WAS AT THE SAME TIME** assuring his less broad-minded brethren in the Ministerium of Pennsylvania that his teaching was based entirely on that of Luther.[67]

Whatever happened to Buchman's one tenet called "Absolute Honesty"?

7. IS ALCOHOLISM A DISEASE?

Medical doctors, psychiatrists, psychologists, hospital personnel, and Christian leaders tell us that alcoholism is a disease or an illness. Book after book after book reiterates this opinion and some even refer to alcoholism as an allergy.[1] The *Encyclopedia Britannica* indicates that alcoholism "is a disease in which a person has an uncontrollable desire for alcohol."[2] One pamphlet expresses this idea in these words:

> Today we are willing to accept the idea that, as far as we are concerned, alcoholism is an illness, progressive illness which can never be "cured," but which, like some other illnesses, *can* be arrested. We agree that there is nothing shameful about having an illness, provided we face the problem honestly and try to do something about it. We are perfectly willing to admit that we are allergic to alcohol and that it is simply common sense to stay away from the source of our allergy....
>
> We did not know too much about alcoholism....
>
> Most of us, however, were relieved when it was explained to us that alcoholism was an illness. We saw the common sense of doing something about an illness that threatened to destroy us. [Emphasis in the original.][3]

The Power of One Vote

Of course, alcoholism was not always considered to be a disease. At one time (just a few decades ago) it was believed to be a moral failure or a sin. In actuality, this belief that alcoholism is a disease is really a cover-up for the breweries. If we turn our attention to the alcoholics, then our focus is not on alcohol. A number of years ago to help their cause, a malting company gave $80,000 to the Yale School of Alcoholic Studies so that this school would propagate the idea that alcoholism was a disease.[4] Then, in "Powell v. Texas, a 5 to 4 Supreme Court vote determined that alcoholism is a disease."[5] So, even the

Supreme Court has stated that alcoholism is a disease, but the question still remains: "Is alcoholism really a disease OR is it a sin?"

Harold Mulford who is Director of Alcohol Studies at the University of Iowa has stated:

> I think it's important to recognize that the alcohol disease concept is a propaganda and political achievement and not a scientific achievement. Science has not demonstrated that alcoholism is a disease by defining it, nor has science or technology demonstrated it to be a disease by coming up with an effective treatment or preventative.[6]

In other words, the decision to make alcoholism a disease has no medical or scientific basis. Rather, it was decided by a vote. Other diseases have not been dependent on such voting. Had the vote been 4 to 5 instead of 5 to 4, alcoholism would not "officially" be considered a disease. Labeling alcoholism as a disease, however, helps to absolve an alcoholic's guilty conscience. After all, if he has a disease, then his problem drinking cannot be helped. As one pamphlet alleges:

> Alcoholism is a disease, not a moral failure or lack of willpower. As you begin to accept this fact, you'll recognize that much of the alcoholic's behavior results from the illness.[7]

Another pamphlet asserts: "Once alcoholism has set in, there is nothing morally wrong about being ill."[8] So, the alcoholic can now shrug his shoulders and say, "I have a disease and, therefore, anything I do, no matter how wrong it may be, cannot be held against me. I am a sick man and my illness makes me do things I am not accountable for. Don't blame me for what I've done. It's not my fault that I'm an alcoholic. I can't help that I have a disease. You'll just have to understand that I have an allergy which causes me to get into trouble."

No Benefits Gained

Labeling alcoholism as a disease has not benefited anyone, especially the alcoholic; it only hurts him all the more. Rather than helping the problem, this designation merely allows the alcoholic to continue his drinking—only now he has a logical "excuse" why he drinks. What makes matters worse is, if an alcoholic feels he has a disease, then he believes that what he is doing is okay and he sees no need for repentance. After all, you don't have to repent for contracting a disease, so not only is an alcoholic's conscience eased by knowing he has a "disease," he now is cleared from spiritual responsibility because coming down with a disease is not sinful. There is much physical and spiritual harm that has been incurred because alcoholism is now listed as a disease.

Who is susceptible to this "disease" of alcoholism? One AA pamphlet states:

> We in A.A. believe alcoholism is a disease that is no respecter of age, sex, creed, race, wealth, occupation, or education. It strikes at random. Our experience seems to show that *anyone* can be an alcoholic. [Emphasis in the original.][9]

Let's analyze this assessment. Can alcoholism REALLY strike "AT RANDOM?" Can ANYONE be an alcoholic? Of course not! The ONLY way alcoholism can strike and the ONLY way that someone can become an alcoholic is to drink alcoholic beverages. If you do not drink, you have NO chance whatsoever of developing alcoholism.

> Though now it's a disease
> Somewhat akin to colic
> It still takes alcohol
> To make an alcoholic.[10]

So, is alcoholism a disease? Well, if it is,

1. It is the only disease that is contracted by an act of the will;

2. It is the only disease that requires a license to propagate it;

3. It is the only disease that is bottled and sold;

4. It is the only disease that requires outlets to spread it;

5. It is the only disease that produces a revenue for the Government;

6. It is the only disease that provokes crime;

7. It is the only disease that is habit-forming;

8. It is the only disease that brings violent death on the highways;

9. It is the only disease that is spread by advertising;

10. It is the only disease without a germ or virus cause, and for which there is no human corrective medicine;

11. It is the only disease which we are fined for contracting;

12. And last, but not least, it is the only disease that bars the patient from heaven, for no drunkard shall inherit the kingdom of God. (Except there is repentance...1 Cor. 6:9-10). [11]

Diagnosing Alcoholism

How is this "disease" of alcoholism diagnosed? Would you believe that it is usually determined **BY THE ALCOHOLIC** rather than by a physician? Nan Robertson, a former alcoholic who is a member of Alcoholics Anonymous, asks "Who is an alcoholic?" Her response is:

Alcoholism is insidious, baffling, powerful, progressive. It only gets worse, never better. And **YOU CAN'T COUNT ON YOUR DOCTOR** to tell you what's wrong with you: Often your own physician may not detect the cause because you are lying about your drinking, or because he or she knows little more about alcoholism than you do....

HOW CAN YOU TELL if you are an alcoholic? ONLY *YOU* CAN MAKE THAT DECISION. [Emphasis added.][12]

This sure is some disease if "ONLY YOU can make that decision." What other disease can be determined this way? This shows you how "scientific" this theory really is (or isn't)!

Even though it should be plain to see that alcoholism IS NOT a disease, Christian leaders still propagate this falsehood. One Christian psychologist writes in one of his books:

Do not nag, complain, scream, cry, beg, plead, embarrass, label or berate the **victim**. He has a *disease* which he can't control. It is not within his power to overcome it alone. [Emphasis in the original.][13]

Actually, if alcoholism is a disease, it is the easiest "disease" to cure. All one has to do is stay away from alcoholic beverages. Granted, addictions are not easy to overcome, but if one can exercise control, the "disease" can disappear over night; it can reappear just as quickly when control is not exercised. Needless to say, alcoholism is the only disease that can "come and go" time and time again just by taking a drink and then leaving the drink alone. Really, I was unaware that a disease could just come or go dependent on a person's intake of beverages. Diseases such as cancer, measles, mumps, and tuberculosis, certainly are not controlled in any such way.

What other disease is PROMOTED and bragged up to the public? The television, billboards, and magazines carry ads portraying the "glories" of alcoholic beverages. If this is a dreaded disease, why are people trying to encourage it by promotional advertising? Have you ever seen an ad trying to convince you to contract cancer? Did you ever encounter a magazine ad announcing a sale on how to obtain tuberculosis? When was the last time you saw a commercial trying to influence you to buy measles or mumps? The truth of the matter is, alcoholism is not a disease!

Another fascinating factor is that if alcoholism is a disease, it is the only disease that can be eradicated over night by not allowing liquor or any other alcoholic beverage to be sold. What other disease could be done away with so easily? Furthermore, what other disease has buildings constructed throughout the world to manufacture it daily?

A Disease or a Sin?

No, alcoholism IS NOT a disease; it is a sin which is willfully committed by a person. It is true that a person may not be able to easily break the psychological and physical addiction to alcohol, but, nonetheless, the individual still has a choice in saying "yes" or "no" to partaking of alcoholic beverages in the first place. There are many sins that have a tremendous grip on a person, making it extremely difficult to break free from them. Adultery, as well as other sins, hold sway over countless men and women, but just because a habit is hard to break, do we have the right to label it as a "disease"?

Some people are probably wondering: "Why isn't alcoholism a disease? Look at all the suffering and physical problems that go with it." There are many physical afflictions that affect the alcoholic, and alcoholism certainly can (and usually does) cause diseases, but the alcohol itself is not the disease, it is the CAUSE of the disease. Homosexual activity can cause AIDS. AIDS is a disease, but the homosexual activity itself is not a disease. A person's lifestyle can result in sickness, but the lifestyle itself is not the sickness. Sin has consequences and many times our ungodly deeds produce physical ramifications, but our actions cannot be considered as a disease, although these actions may result in individuals coming down with a disease. A disease will not keep us out of heaven, but an ungodly lifestyle will. A person with AIDS can enter heaven IF his sins have been forgiven, but a homosexual cannot (I Corinthians 6:9). A person who has developed cirrhosis of the liver or any other complications from drinking can enter heaven IF he has confessed his sins and repented of them, but a drunkard cannot enter into heaven (I Corinthians 6:9-10). A distinction must be made between a person's lifestyle and actions and his physical condition that may have resulted from his lifestyle. An alcoholic may confess his sins and be forgiven even though he will probably have to live with the consequences of his previous lifestyle which was caused by his sin.

If alcoholism is a medically or scientifically diagnosed disease, why do drunk drivers get fined or have to spend some time in jail? "...approximately a third of *all* police arrests in this country are for drunkenness." [Emphasis in the original.][14] In addition, the Minnesota Council on Alcohol Problems reveals that

> ... alcoholism is associated with 50% to 75% of all crime, child abuse, and highway accidents, also to broken marriages, poverty, child neglect, wife-beating, and suicide, plus cirrhosis of the liver and other diseases.[15]

What other disease is so prevalent and causes so many abuses and heartaches? Clearly, an alcoholic is in a predicament, but he does not have a disease. His problem is called SIN.

Man says sin is:	God says sin is:
Acceptable	Abominable (II Kings 21:11)
Benign	Beguiling (II Corinthians 11:3)
Carelessness	Condemnation (Romans 5:18)
Desirous	Disobedience (Romans 5:19)
Entertainment	Evilness (I Kings 14:22)
Funny	Foolishness (Proverbs 24:9)
Good	Grievous (Genesis 18:20)
Harmless	Horrible (Jeremiah 23:14)
Ignorance	Iniquity (Psalm 51:2)

Justifiable	Japery (mockery) (Proverbs 14:9)
Kooky	Knavery (dishonesty) (II Corinthians 4:2)
Legitimate	Lewdness (Ezekiel 23:49)
Meaningless	Maliciousness (Romans 1:29)
Nonsense	Negligence (Hebrews 2:3)
Okay	Obstinacy (stubbornness) (I Samuel 15:23)
Permissible	Provoking (I Kings 16:13)
Quaint	Quarantinable (it will keep us out of heaven) (Revelation 21:27)
Reasonable	Rebellion (I Samuel 15:23)
Silly	Sinful (Romans 7:13)
Trivial	Transgressing (I John 3:4)
Understandable	Unrighteousness (I John 5:17)
Venial	Vexation (II Peter 2:7-8)
Wittiness	Wickedness (Genesis 39:9)
Xciting	Xasperating (Hebrews 3:9-10)
Yore (in the past)	Yielding (Romans 6:13-16)
Zany	Zealousness (Galatians 4:17)

Many people today believe that sin is an old-fashioned word and make a joke of it as can be seen by a bumper sticker that reads: "I didn't invent sin: I'm just trying to perfect it." The Bible, however, tells us that "FOOLS make a mock at sin..." (Proverbs 14:9). You can see God views sin a lot differently (and far more seriously) than individuals do.

Effectiveness of AA

AA promotes the fallacy that alcoholism is a disease and states that this principle is one of the tenets of its organization.[16] Since AA is based on a dilapidated and crumbling foundation, let's see how effective its treatment program is. AA endorser and member, Nan Robertson, informs us that

> About 60 percent of all newcomers—some still drinking at first, most not—who go to meetings for up to a year remain in A.A. Usually, they stay sober for good. That means, of course, that 40 percent are lost to A.A. after trying out its program. These statistics refute the widely held notion of outsiders that Alcoholics Anonymous is successful with everyone.[17]

Notice that Robertson said that about 40 percent are lost to AA. These figures may be much higher, however, because she qualifies her statement with the remark that about 60 percent of those who attend AA FOR UP TO A YEAR continue on. How many are lost to AA who do not stick around for that year?

Another writer reveals the research of William Miller and Reid Hester on the effectiveness (or noneffectiveness) of AA:

> In spite of the fact that it inspires nearly universal acclaim and enthusiasm among alcoholism treatment personnel in the United States, Alcoholics Anonymous (A.A.) wholly lacks experimental support for its efficacy....

> Only two studies have employed random assignment and adequate controls to compare the efficacy of A.A. versus no intervention or alternative interventions. Brandsma *et al.* (1980) found NO DIFFERENCES at 12-month follow-up between A.A. and no treatment, and at 3-month follow-up those assigned to A.A. were found to be significantly MORE likely to be binge drinking, relative to controls or those assigned to other interventions (based on unverified self-reports). Ditman and Crawford (1966) assigned court mandated "alcohol addicts" to A.A., clinic treatment, or no treatment (probation only). Based

on records of rearrest, 31% of A.A. clients and 32% of clinic-treated clients were judged successful, as compared with 44% success in the untreated group (Ditman, Crawford, Forgy, Moskowitz, & MacAndrew, 1967). [Emphasis added.][18]

Dr. Stanton Peele, who is a senior health researcher at Mathematica Policy Research and author of *Diseasing of America: Addiction Treatment Out of Control,* says "Several studies have shown that those who quit drinking via A.A. actually have **HIGHER RELAPSE RATES** than those who quit on their own." [Emphasis added.][19]

So, although the AA treatment program is expounded as an effective means of arresting alcoholism, the facts prove otherwise.

8. "GAINS" AND LOSSES OF ALCOHOLISM

Alcoholism in America has cost a tremendous amount in financial loss to the alcoholics' families, employers, and in loss of human lives. Let's look a few statistics.

• There are 10.6 million adult alcoholics in America with another 7.3 million adults who have serious alcohol abuse problems. These 17.9 million people affect another 56 million people directly.[1]

• The average age for a person to start drinking is 12. They are usually introduced to alcoholic beverages by their own parents.[2]

• One survey indicated that over fifty percent of teenagers who drink learned to drink at home.[3]

• According to one study of 65,000 students, 75 percent of the high school seniors drink beer.[4] Another survey taken at a state university revealed that 95 percent of those surveyed drank.[5]

• Alcohol is the leading killer of young people, claiming the lives of some 10,000 young people between the ages of 16 and 24 annually.[6]

• "Before turning 18, the average child will see 75,000 drinking scenes on television programs."[7]

• America's #1 drug problem among youth is alcohol.[8]

• Alcohol usually leads to other drug use. "A survey of 27,000 seventh to twelfth graders in New York State found little or no use of other drugs among teens who had not used alcohol first."[9]

• Cigarette smoking is associated with alcoholism—over 90 percent of all alcoholics also smoke.[10]

• Suicide is attempted more frequently by teens who use alcohol or drugs. According to *The Fifth Special Report to the*

U.S. Congress on Alcohol and Health (1983), as many as 80 percent of people who attempt suicide have been drinking at the time.[11]

• More than 50 percent of college students who confessed to engaging in violent crimes admitted that they were high on alcohol or drugs when the crime was committed.[12]

• Between 100,000 and 200,000 people die each year from misuse of alcohol.[13]

• Alcohol is associated with 54 percent of all violent crimes.[14]

• Close to half of all deaths from traffic accidents are alcohol-related.[15]

• In America alone, there are 70 deaths **EVERY DAY** due to alcohol-related traffic accidents.[16]

• "The annual cost of alcoholism is $89.5 billion for treatment and indirect losses such as reduced worker productivity, early death and property damage resulting from alcohol-related accidents and crime each year."[17]

• Alcohol is responsible for up to 40 percent of industrial fatalities and 47 percent of industrial injuries.[18]

• In addition to highway accidents, alcohol is responsible for about six million non-fatal and 15,000 fatal injuries in the home, at play and in public places.[19]

• "Alcohol is closely connected to the four leading causes of accidental death in the US: auto crashes (about half are alcohol-related), falls (17- 53%),[20] drownings (69 %), and fires (83%)."[21]

• In 1975, the state of Illinois lowered its legal drinking age from 21 to 18. In just two years' time, the drink-related crimes which were committed by the youth increased so drastically that Illinois planned on moving the age limit back up to 21.[22]

• "Sixty-nine per cent of our police force is maintained because of drink. Our liquor bill in one year would build two million homes. There are three pubs for every church in our nation. Every fifth home must furnish a boy to fill the liquor factories."[23]

Results of Prohibition

Some people claim that Prohibition never worked and that it was for the best that Prohibition was repealed. Regardless of this assertion, let's look at some facts:

During prohibition the general death-rate for alcoholism fell to 19% of the pre-prohibition rate.

The death-rate for cirrhosis of the liver fell 54.3%.

During the prohibition years the death-rate was at a lower level than in any single year before prohibition.

Admissions for alcoholic psychosis to mental hospitals were lower after introduction of prohibition than for any previous similar period.

The tuberculosis death-rate fell at all ages during prohibition.

There was an actual increase in the savings, insurance policies and assets of building and loan associations per capita at a rate not previously experienced.

There was less brutality to and neglect of children in the homes.

The conditions of the aged and infirm improved.

There was a great increase in per capita consumption of milk products.[24]

For the industrial worker the "blue Monday" was practically eliminated, industrial accidents decreased and work efficiency records improved....

Many hospitals for "alcohol cure" were closed. County jails were practically empty.[25]

Effects of Alcoholism

Not only does the alcoholic hurt others, his own body will bear serious consequences. Alcoholism causes major health problems. "In the U.S., it is the third great killer, after heart disease and cancer...."[26]

Long-term, heavy drinking can cause dementia, in which the individual loses memory and the ability to think abstractly, to recall names of common objects, to use correct words to describe recognized objects or to follow simple instructions.[27]

Continued excessive drinking produces a number of disagreeable physical symptoms that add to the alcoholic's anxiety.... The lining of the stomach and intestines becomes inflamed so that food is not easily digested. Furthermore, morning nausea renders any food unpalatable, and the alcoholic therefore may take two or three drinks on arising in order to overcome his nausea and anxiety. With the loss of essential dietary constituents the alcoholic begins to show signs of food deficiencies. His nerves, particularly those in his legs, may undergo degeneration, giving rise to pain and weakness. The liver suffers severe changes, grouped by physicians under the term cirrhosis. The organ is enlarged, the person's skin darkens as he becomes jaundiced, the abdominal cavity swells as it fills with fluid. Sometimes the patient dies in a coma as a result of failure of liver function. He suffers severe headaches, dizziness, nausea and vomiting, the well-known hangover symptoms. These symptoms are partly due to gastritis, or inflammation of the lining of the stomach, but they are also a direct effect of alcohol on the inner ear, the part of that organ that aids in regulating the equilibrium of the body. The characteristic thirst is ascribed to loss of fluids through perspiration, urination and vomiting.[28]

Alcoholism surely is a problem which causes pain, heartache, and death, but aren't there any benefits that can come about because of alcohol? Actually, there are a number of items that an alcoholic can gain through his drinking. I've made a list of some of these "gains" as well as some of the losses of an alcoholic lifestyle:

"GAINS"	LOSSES
Pain	Alertness
Poverty	Reasoning
Sickness	Job
Disease	Family
Redness of eyes, nose, and face	Friends
Memory lapses	Respect from others
Sorrow	Home
Embarrassment	Money
Shame	Health
Dullness of mind	Character
Disgrace	Happiness
Crime	Life
Accidents	Reputation
Hangovers	Food
Death	Clothes
Tremors of the hands	Coordination
Jail	Morals
Tragedy	HEAVEN
Jaundice	
Despair	
Palsy	

Insanity

Paralysis of muscles

Epilepsy

Burning in hands and feet

Anemia

Heart Disease

Cirrhosis of the liver

Malnutrition

Nerve and muscle damage

Quarrels

Heartaches

Tears

Remorse

HELL

Although you may not gain all of the above, one thing that ALL alcoholics will gain is HELL.

Although you may not experience all of the above, losses, one loss that ALL alcoholics will have is HEAVEN

Below is a poem that describes more consequences of an alcoholic lifestyle. It was written by a life convict in the Joliet Prison in reference to a saloon (bar):

> A Bar to heaven, a door to hell;
>> Whoever named it, named it well.
> A Bar to manliness and wealth;
>> A door to want and broken health.

A Bar to honor, pride and fame;
   A door to grief and sin and shame.
A Bar to hope, a bar to prayer;
   A door to darkness and despair.
A Bar to honored useful life;
   A door to brawling, senseless strife
A Bar to all that's true and brave;
   A door to every drunkard's grave.
A Bar to joys that home imparts;
   A door to tears and aching hearts.
A Bar to heaven, a door to hell;
   Whoever named it, named it well.[29]

Statistics show that ten thousand people are killed by liquor for every one killed by a mad dog. Yet the authorities shoot the dog and license the liquor! Alcoholism is five times more prevalent than cancer, twenty-two times more prevalent than tuberculosis, and a hundred times more prevalent than polio. Yet Americans spend millions annually to fight cancer, tuberculosis, and polio, while doling out only pennies to combat liquor![30]

Someone has stated: "The gunman wants 'your money or your life.' The tavern takes both."[31]

"If Only…"

With all the sorrow and sickness that is often associated with drinking, why do people drink? One excuse that is given is that the circumstances were so bad that the person was driven to drink. "If only you would live with my wife, you'd drink, too," or "If you would have gone through a painful childhood like I did, you'd be an alcoholic," are some of the "reasons" that you've probably heard. Here is one story of such an excuse:

Two men bumped into each other one day in a railway

station in Austria. One was an alcoholic, begging for enough money to buy one more bottle of rum. The other man asked him how he got in that condition—existing from one drink to another. The beggar responded that from the beginning, the cards of life had been stacked against him. His mother had died when he was very young; his father had beaten him and his brothers and sisters mercilessly. Then World War I came along and the family was separated. "You see," explained the beggar, "I never had a chance. If you had grown up as I did, you would be this way, too."

The other man replied, "This is very strange. The truth of the matter is that my background is very similar to yours. I, too, lost my mother when I was young. My father was also a brutal man, often beating me and my brothers and sisters. The war also separated me from my family. However, I felt I had no choice but to try to overcome these circumstances rather than being overcome by them."

As the two men continued their conversation they made a remarkable discovery. They were, in fact, blood brothers, long separated by the trauma of war!

Two human beings came out of the identical set of circumstances, yet one ended with a life of excellence and the other with a life of despair. I suspect that our most powerful ally in difficult circumstances is simply the realization that we can choose how we react.[32]

Yes, some of the circumstances can be very discouraging. Many people have grown up in a home of abuse, incest, drunkenness, divorce, or with other frustrating and perplexing problems. Many, it seemed, had no chance to amount to anything. Other people have severe illnesses and handicaps that are against them, but some have a determination to make it through life and others just give up and look for excuses. Then, there are those who had every advantage possible in life and still end up as an alcoholic. Our circumstances really don't play as much a part in our lives as some individuals like to think. Certainly our childhood does affect us to some extent, but what has happened in the past has happened. The only choices we really have are to cave in to the circumstances and continue to live a worthless life and make a miserable life for our partner and our children as well, **or** to move forward and to overlook and overcome our hurts. It may be easier said than done, I realize, but with God "all things are possible" (Mark 10:27).

9. ADULT CHILDREN OF ALCOHOLICS

Alcoholics Anonymous dates the start of their organization from June 1935. In 1951, Lois Wilson, the wife of AA co-founder, Bill Wilson, launched Al-Anon. Al-Anon is for any person who has a friend or loved one who was or is an alcoholic. Over 15,000 Al-Anon groups are in the United States alone with more than 13,000 other groups worldwide. Alateen was also started in the 1950's. "Al-Anon/Alateen meetings encourage recognition of alcoholism as a disease...."[1] "The factor that unifies Al-Anon and Alateens' world-wide groups is a set of principles derived from Alcoholics Anonymous, known as the Twelve Steps."[2]

Another fellowship that began in 1981 was called Adult Children of Alcoholics. "There were fourteen Adult Children groups registered with Al-Anon headquarters in 1981, and 1,000 by 1986."[3] The Adult Children of Alcoholics are known as ACAs, ACOAs, or COAs. As their name suggests, those who attend ACA meetings are individuals who as children were raised in an alcoholic home. ACA, like Al-Anon and Alateen, have their programs based on the Twelve Steps of AA which we covered previously.

> Like the pioneers of Alcoholics Anonymous and Al-Anon before them, the members are groping. Someone unfamiliar with the Adult Children but knowledgeable about A.A. or Al-Anon may be unsettled by the rage. It is directed not just against the drunken father who raised them but also against the nonalcoholic mother—the martyr, the scold, the dominator.[4]

Expressing all this rage is not only not Christ-like, it is not making matters any better for the individual manifesting the anger. It may help someone to unburden himself temporarily, but the anger is still pent-up and the more times the issue is rehearsed, the more embedded in one's mind it becomes. Dwelling on one's past hurts will not change those hurts. In fact, thinking about the hurts only makes their memories linger much longer, creates more anger and bitterness, and ends up hurting the individual even more. The Bible tells us:

> Finally, brethren, whatsoever things are true, whatsoever things are honest, whatsoever things are just, whatsoever things are pure, whatsoever things are lovely, whatsoever things are of good report; if there be any virtue, and if there be any praise, think on these things (Philippians 4:8).

We are to focus our thoughts on things that are pure, true, honest, lovely, just, and of good report, not on things that torment and hurt us. Paul also encourages us to FORGET "those things which are behind" (Philippians 3:13).

Joseph's "Raw Deal"

One illustration that is recorded in the Bible is about Joseph. He was dearly loved of his father, but his brothers were very jealous of him. One day, in obedience to his father, he went to see how his brothers were doing. When the brothers saw him coming, they plotted together and planned to kill him. One brother, Reuben, talked the other boys out of the evil scheme, and they threw him into a pit instead. In the meantime, a caravan of Ishmeelites passed through and Joseph's brothers decided to sell him to them. Joseph was then sold into Egypt unto Potiphar. Because of his excellent conduct, he was promoted, but the promotion brought a problem. His master's wife desired to have Joseph commit fornication with her and, when he refused, she lied about him and accused him of trying to seduce her. This untruth landed Joseph in prison. After several years he was finally released and eventually became a ruler in Egypt. Yes, Joseph had some good times and promotions, but he also suffered a great deal. When his first child was born he named him Manasseh, meaning "forgetting," "For God, said he, hath made me forget all my toil, and all my father's house" (Genesis 41:51). Instead of dwelling on his misfortunes, bemoaning the fact that he was alone and without family or friends in a strange land, he made the best of the situation, behaved himself properly, and picked up the pieces of his life and went forward.

Joseph could have blamed God for allowing the pain, loneliness, and imprisonment to happen, but he was thankful **IN SPITE OF** his circumstances. Instead of complaining, he was praising God for the good that came his way. Granted, Joseph was not an ACA, but he did have hurts that he could have held onto and talked about. When his brothers came into Egypt because a famine was in their own land, they stood before Joseph. They did not know that the ruler they were requesting food from was the brother whom they had plotted to kill about 20 years previously. When Joseph recognized them, instead of trying to get even and turning them away without food, he even returned their money along with the food. Joseph could have told the servants how his brothers had treated him and how they had planned to kill him, but he knew that the situation could not be changed, so why should he spend his time thinking about the "raw deal" he got when he could fill his mind with encouraging and worthwhile thoughts?

Life in a Drunkard's Home

I was raised in a good Christian home so I didn't experience the suffering firsthand of being an ACA. My mother, on the other hand, does know how it feels to be an ACA. She was raised in a drunkard's home where both parents drank. In fact, her father was the "town drunk." She felt the hurt when the bartender's son would come to school and make fun of her and tell the other children about how her father acted in the bar. She knows the fear of being in her parents' car as they swerved from lane to lane because they were too drunk to know which side of the road they were supposed to be on. Her heart was broken time and again as promises were made to her by drunken parents only to have them back down on the promises later on. She remembers when her father tried to break every bone in her mother's body and she felt the pain in her own body as she was thrown across the kitchen floor when she tried to go for help. Yes, she knows the agony of being an ACA firsthand.

What can she do about these bitter memories? She really only had two choices. She could dwell on them and build up hate and resentment, or she could make the best of a bad situation, pick up the pieces, and go on. What choice did she make? She chose to leave the past behind her, take her hurts and heartaches to the Lord, and go forward. No, she is not denying that the past happened to her; she is not refusing to admit that these things took place, but she is refusing to rehash the same situations over and over and over again. She is refusing to allow her past to control and ruin her present and her future. Thinking about her past will only keep opening wounds that could otherwise heal.

What caused her to come through this so well? She heard the message of salvation and accepted Jesus Christ as her personal Lord and Savior. He took care of the healing process in her life. Through placing her trust in Christ, my mother no longer needed to drag the unnecessary baggage of her past with her. Not only did she find healing, but at the same altar of prayer her mother also found the Lord and never touched a cigarette or drink of alcohol from that night on. Her mother found that "If we confess our sins, He is faithful and just to forgive us our sins, and to cleanse us from all unrighteousness" (I John 1:9). Not every one can leave the past behind so easily but my grandmother had a great faith and love for the Lord and believed that He could give her an immediate deliverance from alcohol and He honored her faith. There is healing for both the alcoholic and the ACA, but too many times we fail to recognize the real source of this healing power: Jesus Christ.

What Is Visualization?

While ACAs may find comfort in attending ACA meetings where other people have gone through some of the same hurts as they have, the problem still remains that the situations of the past cannot be changed. Some people, many of whom may be well-meaning, are advocating visualization and inner healing to try to change an individual's hurtful past. One book dealing with this subject is by Daryl E. Quick, entitled *The Healing Journey for Adult Children of Alcoholics*. Daryl was an ACA, and in trying to help others, he gives several visualization techniques in his book for ACAs to practice. The trouble with this approach, however, is that visualization and inner healing methods are OCCULT practices that have been used by witches, shamans (witchdoctors), and other occultists for thousands of years. Practicing these exercises will only harm the already hurting person even moreso. At first, some relief may take place and may seem to bring a "healing of the memories," but involvement in occult procedures only leads to entanglement in an evilly-devised system of Satanic bondage. Many have tried to "Christianize" these overtly occultic methods, but we cannot take an evil practice and turn it into something that is holy and good. You can't "Christianize" Satanism, neither can you "Christianize" visualization and inner healing. The sad thing is that these techniques have been introduced into the church in recent years. In fact, Daryl Quick's book is sold through "Christian" bookstores.

Although it is beyond the scope of this book to go into detail on visualization, we will briefly touch on it here.[5] One WITCH explains that "visualization includes not only vision but sound, smell, taste, touch, movement and emotion."[6] One New Age book suggests: "Visualize as many details— sights, sounds, smells, and feelings—as you need to CREATE A SCENE SO REAL, your body becomes CONVINCED it's happening." [Emphasis added.][7] The purpose of visualization is to CHANGE the PRESENT or PAST CIRCUM-STANCES and to "create your own reality." New Agers themselves tell us that this technique "is a simple yet potent form of MAGICK." [Emphasis added.][8]

An example of how visualization would be used for an ACA would be for the ACA to think of one particularly painful memory.

Perhaps the person remembers a brutal beating from a drunken mother or father. The individual tries to recreate this scene in the memory in as much detail as possible, including the colors of the clothing that was worn at that time, the sounds of the screaming, the sight of the blood oozing, the pain of the wounds, etc. As the scene progresses, this individual is to visualize another person or guide coming into the picture. The guide can be a childhood or an imaginary friend, an animal, or even "Jesus."

This friend is then perceived in the imagination as helping to heal the situation. The friend could be visualized as intervening and stopping the fighting, bandaging the wounds, and caressing the child. The entire scene is played out in the ACA's mind and the ACA (or anyone else who is practicing visualization) is taught that even though the incident is occurring in the imagination, in reality the situation is also being changed. "Visualization is the essence of the ABILITY OF BENDING REALITY to will." [Emphasis added.][9] Bending reality is what MAGIC is all about.

An Altered State

What is wrong with visualization? Actually, what takes place during a visualization session is what makes it wrong. A person may start by visualizing an imaginary scene (or a real one that can be remembered from the past), but what eventually transpires while one is in this ALTERED STATE OF CONSCIOUSNESS is that CONTACT is made with so-called spirit guides which are in reality DEMONS! Even when visualization is used for easing pain or unfavorable memories, these spirit guides are contacted. (By the way, other terms for a "spirit guide" include, but are not limited to: imaginary guide, inner guide, imaginary doctor, guide, inner adviser, wise old man, etc., etc.)

Those who have tried to "Christianize" visualization tell you to visualize or imagine "Jesus" as your spirit guide, but in both the

"Christianized" variation and the occultic version, the IMAGE that YOU CONJURE UP ends up eventually TALKING WITH YOU! A demonic spirit guide, Soli, tells us (like many so-called "Christians") that it DOESN'T MATTER how we visualize the guides for "However YOU PERCEIVE of us in the spirit dimension, THAT is how WE WILL APPEAR to you." [Emphasis added.][10] So, even though a person may visualize a "Jesus," the demonic spirit guide is the one that materializes—only it **APPEARS** to be Jesus! No matter which method is used, the so-called "Christian" form of visualization or the occultic version, the fact remains: *"The same technique of visualization used to allegedly encounter Jesus is used in occultism for the purpose of contacting spirit guides."* [Emphasis in the original.][11] Besides, the Bible tells us that "we walk by FAITH, NOT by SIGHT" (II Corinthians 5:7). Visualization and inner healing are methods that endeavor to nullify God's Word because those who ensue these practices are walking by SIGHT rather than by FAITH.

Instead of placing our hope and trust in man (and in the case of visualization, demons!), why don't we just take our burdens to the Lord and leave them with Him? One songwriter appropriately penned the following:

> Does Jesus care when my heart is pained
> Too deeply for mirth and song;
> As the burdens press, and the cares distress,
> And the way grows weary and long?
> Does Jesus care when my way is dark
> With a nameless dread and fear?
> As the daylight fades into deep night shades,
> Does He care enough to be near?
>
> O yes, He cares—I know He cares!
> His heart is touched with my grief;
> When the days are weary, the long nights dreary,
> I know my Savior cares.[12]

The Bible bears this out: "Casting all your care upon Him; for He careth for you" (I Peter 5:7). Let's not carry our own burdens. As another songwriter stated:

> My Jesus knows when I am lonely,
> He knows each pain, He sees each tear;
> He understands each lonely heartache,
> He understands because He cares.[13]

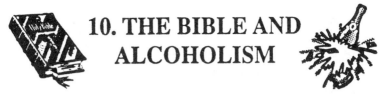

10. THE BIBLE AND ALCOHOLISM

The following statement is read at many Alcoholics Anonymous meetings: "A.A...does not wish to engage in any controversy, NEITHER ENDORSES NOR OPPOSES any causes." [Emphasis added.][1] Furthermore, AA

> ...takes NO POSITION on the so-called temperance question. Collectively, its members neither approve nor disapprove the use of alcohol by others. They have simply learned from experience that they cannot handle alcohol themselves. [Emphasis added.][2]

Although each AA member may be free to decide where he stands on the alcohol issue, AA literature states:

> While many A.A.'s appreciate that alcohol may be all right for most people, they know it to be poison for them. The average A.A. has no desire to deprive anyone of something that, properly handled, is a source of pleasure. The A.A. merely acknowledges being personally unable to handle the stuff.[3]

Though AA collectively may not take sides on the issue of alcohol, the co-founders of AA definitely let it be known where they stood on this subject. Neither Bill Wilson nor Bob Smith were against alcohol in any way. In fact, both of these men purchased alcohol for others. Bill explains his views like this:

> Assuming we are spiritually fit, we can do all sorts of things alcoholics are not supposed to do. People have said we must not go where liquor is served; we must not have it in our homes; we must shun friends who drink; we must avoid moving pictures which show drinking scenes; we must not go into bars; our friends must hide their bottles if we go to their houses; we mustn't think or be reminded about alcohol at all. Our experience shows that THIS IS NOT NECESSARILY SO....

So OUR RULE IS NOT TO AVOID a place where there is drinking, *if we have a legitimate reason for being there.* That includes bars, nightclubs, dances, receptions, weddings, even plain ordinary whoopee parties. To a person who has had experience with an alcoholic, this may seem like tempting Providence, but it isn't....

IF YOU ARE WITH A PERSON WHO WANTS TO EAT IN A BAR, BY ALL MEANS GO ALONG....

MANY OF US KEEP LIQUOR IN OUR HOMES. We often need it to carry green recruits through a severe hangover. Some of us still serve it to our friends provided they are not alcoholic....

WE ARE CAREFUL NEVER TO SHOW INTOLERANCE OR HATRED OF DRINKING AS AN INSTITUTION.... Every new alcoholic looks for this spirit among us and is immensely relieved when he finds we are not witchburners. A spirit of intolerance might repel alcoholics whose lives could have been saved, had it not been for such stupidity. [Italics in the original. Bold and capitals added.][4]

Even though AA claims that they neither endorse nor oppose any cause, it should be obvious that this is not the case. It is undoubtedly evident that AA does endorse drinking in spite of the fact that they believe alcoholics should not drink. In addition, it should be noted that those who do oppose drink are labeled as stupid and intolerant by Bill Wilson.[5]

Biblical View of Alcoholism

A Christian's guidebook is the Bible. Does the Bible condemn, condone, or remain silent on this issue? The Bible, unlike AA's inaccurate assertion, does take a stand on this matter. In fact, the Bible has a lot to say about this subject. There are well over 200 references to "wine," not to mention many other references to "strong drink" and "drunkenness," etc. The Bible records many instances where people did drink intoxicating beverages and some of the results. Drunkenness was the cause of incest (Genesis 19:31-38), nakedness (Genesis 9:21-23), and being led into a death trap (II Samuel 13:28; 1 Kings 16:8-10 1 Kings 20:13-21).

In another place the Bible gives an accurate description of a drunkard:

Who hath woe? who hath sorrow? who hath contentions? who hath babbling? who hath wounds without cause? who hath redness of eyes?

They that tarry long at the wine; they that go to seek mixed wine.

Look not thou upon the wine when it is red, when it giveth his colour in the cup, when it moveth itself aright.

At the last it biteth like a serpent, and stingeth like an adder.

Thine eyes shall behold strange women, and thine heart shall utter perverse things.

Yea, thou shalt be as he that lieth down in the midst of the sea, or as he that lieth upon the top of a mast.

They have stricken me, shalt thou say, and I was not sick; they have beaten me, and I felt it not: when shall I awake? I will seek it yet again (Proverbs 23:29-35).

Did you notice that the Bible states that the drunkard will have woe, sorrow, contentions, babbling, redness of eyes, and wounds without cause? Isn't this so true? How many people who are not even considered alcoholics have many of these symptoms? How many start "babbling" or become incoherent after a few drinks? How many start to "utter perverse things?" Regardless of the consequences, the Bible accurately indicates that the drunkard will continue to seek out more drink. Notice that just as soon as he awakens he will seek it again. We are told: "Wine is a mocker, strong drink is raging: and WHOSOEVER is deceived thereby is not wise" (Proverbs 20:1).

Not only does the Bible mention the results of drinking, but it also gives a warning in Habakkuk 2:15: "Woe unto him that giveth his neighbour drink, that puttest thy bottle to him, and makest him drunken also...."

Many examples can be found in the Bible where people were forbidden to drink or where drink was refused. The Lord blessed Daniel and his three friends when they refused to partake of the king's wine (Daniel 1:8-20). When Christ was crucified, He was offered "wine mingled with myrrh: but He received it not" (Mark 15:23). One of the requirements for a bishop is that he be "not given to wine" (I Timothy 3:3; Titus 1:7). Aaron and his sons were forbidden to drink wine or strong drink when they went into the tabernacle and this was to be "a statute for ever throughout [their] generations" (Leviticus 10:9).

What about Social Drinking?

Some people may be asking, "Is it all right to drink if I don't get drunk? A social drink now and then won't hurt, will it?" Let's consider some facts. First of all, a woe is pronounced upon ANYONE who gives his neighbor drink. This would include the bartender or the liquor store owner or worker who sells the beverages. Even though he may sell drink to a "social drinker" who does not intend to get drunk, how many alcoholics started out with the idea of becoming an alcoholic? "*Every alcoholic was once—presumably—a social drinker.*" [Emphasis in the original.][6] Their intentions are not to end up lying in the gutter on skid row somewhere. They want to be "respectable" drinkers.

A surprising fact is revealed by one ten-year study which was conducted at Cleveland, Ohio, by Dr. S. R. Gerber. This survey indicated that over 50 percent of the automobile fatalities were caused by drinking drivers, but more "startling still, this study revealed that the **GREATEST NUMBER OF KILLERS AT THE WHEEL**

belonged to the group of so-called 'MODERATE' DRINKERS."
[Emphasis added.][7]

Another question that needs to be asked is: "How many alcoholics became alcoholics without ever drinking?" You know as well as I do that **NOT ONE** individual **EVER** became an alcoholic without first partaking of an alcoholic beverage in one form or another. So, a "social drinker" runs the risk of becoming an alcoholic while a total abstainer will never have to worry about becoming an alcoholic.

An additional point that needs to be considered is: How many drinks can a person have before becoming drunk? The figures vary depending on the body size of the drinker, if any food is eaten with the drink, physical tolerance, the type of beverage consumed, and how fast the beverage is swallowed.[8] Since the figures do differ, for sake of convenience, let's assume that a person must drink six glasses of beer before getting completely intoxicated. What happens if this "social drinker" only takes two glasses of beer? Would you believe that this individual is already two-sixth drunk or over 33 percent intoxicated! Even though a "social drinker" does not intend to become drunk and may be able to stop after two drinks, this person is nonetheless partially drunk. So, even if the "social drinker" can control his drinking intake, he is still on his way to becoming drunk. Additionally, after only two bottles of beer or two shots of whiskey, a person's judgment is already becoming slightly impaired and his reactions are slightly slowed.[9] The Bible explicitly tells us that Christians are to be sober (I Thessalonians 5:6-8) and when a person is partially drunk he is not sober.

Your Influence on Your Children

Furthermore, what influence is the "social drinker" leaving on the family? Are the children being taught that it is okay to drink because mom and dad drink? How many of these children will end up as alcoholics even though their parents were only social drinkers? Our influence is also important. One story I read entitled "Death in the Bottle: The Confessions of a Moderate Drinker" is a case in point. This man went to a Dr. and told him his story of how he had been a heavy drinker in his younger days but said that when he got married he settled down quite a bit and became just a social drinker. At this point in his confession his

> ...voice suddenly became hard and scornful. "Social drinking!" he repeated, in a tone filled with utter loathing, "why, that's the most insidious, damnable, seductive phrase ever coined by Satan. Social drinking was what led my boy Roger to Chicago... yes, he died there in a flophouse on skid row without a friend to comfort him. That's what social drinking did for him!..."[10]

Roger's death had such an impact on the man that he put the drink out of the house so that his other two children wouldn't see it, but he still had to have his drinks "on the sly" because he had become addicted to it. One night his daughter Dorothy came home drunk, so for the first time he told her what had really happened to her brother and begged her to promise him that she would never touch alcohol again. Dorothy did promise, but one night she went to a dance with a very popular guy. The hour was getting quite late but Dorothy had not yet come home. Then the phone rang with some bad news. It was the Sheriff giving the terrible pronouncement that Dorothy had been killed in an accident. At the morgue the father asked the Sheriff if Dorothy and her boyfriend, Rodney, were drinking. The Sheriff replied that Rodney had been but, as far as they could determine, Dorothy had not been. The father finishes the story like this:

> I stumbled back out into the night and began the long drive back home. My jangled nerves cried for relief, but I knew that sleep wouldn't come easily. From a habit of many years, I began to think of the temporary peace a slug of whiskey would bring me. As soon as I reached home, I stumbled from the car and staggered wearily into the living room. Once there, I quickly opened the cupboard where I had kept a bottle of whiskey for

many months. It wasn't there! In its place I saw a slip of white paper. Seizing it, I read the following.

"Rodney forgot his bottle, Father, so we borrowed yours for the night. Don't worry, I won't take any of it."

The note was signed: "Dorothy."[11]

Not only was this the "confession" of a social drinker, it was the legacy that he left to his family. It was **HIS** bottle of whiskey that he had that killed his daughter. What influence are **YOU** having on your family and friends when you claim that social drinking is all right?

Water into Wine

Many people who don't care about what the Bible teaches in most areas will still try to justify their drinking by using the Bible. One example they like to point to is the miracle that Jesus performed at Cana of Galilee where He turned the water into wine. They reason that if Jesus could make wine, then it is okay to drink it, but did Jesus really turn water into an alcoholic beverage? To discover the answer, we must turn our attention to the Hebrew and Greek languages—the languages from which the Old and New Testaments were translated.

... in some cases the word "WINE" in the Bible means a NON-intoxicant, or a FOOD! Fresh grape-juice, to make it keep without fermentation, was boiled until it became thick, like molasses, and in that form was stored away in large jars for future use, to be eaten spread upon bread, or mixed and stirred up in water to make a drink. [Emphasis in the original.][12]

Wine can also mean grape juice, both in the Bible and in secular writings. A few examples from secular sources are:

Varro speaks of "hanging wine."

Cato of "hanging wine" (grapes on the vine).

Columella of "unintoxicating good wine."

Ovid says: "And scarce can the grapes contain the wine they have within."

Ibycus says: "And the new born clusters teem with wine, beneath the shadowy foliage of the vine."

Goethe beautifully says: "And bending down, the grapes o'erflow with wine into the vat below." [13]

Clearly, then, when the word "wine" is mentioned in the Bible it does not always refer to an intoxicating beverage.

The word *oinos* [the Greek word for wine] is used to denote ANY drink made from ANY fruit or vegetable concoctions,—dates, apples, pears, grapes, barley, etc. This in itself is no proof that this wine [at Cana of Galilee] was intoxicating. It could be or it could not be according to the circumstances.

In this instance let us remember that the Lord Jesus Christ is the One who performed the miracle. If this wine is intoxicating then Christ would be under a curse according to Habakkuk 2:15, 16: "Woe unto him that giveth his neighbour drink, that puttest thy bottle to him, and makest him drunken also...."

Furthermore, if this wine of John 2 is intoxicating, then Christ encouraged the people to break the commandment of God. We read in Proverbs 23:31: "Look not thou upon the wine when it is red, when it giveth his colour in the cup, when it moveth itself aright. At the last (Yes, the liquor advertisements never tell us about 'the last' with its poverty, broken lives and broken homes) it biteth like a serpent and stingeth like an adder." [Emphasis in the original.][14]

"Use a Little Wine"

Another verse many people like to use is found in I Timothy 5:23. Here we find that Paul told Timothy: "Drink no longer water, but use a little wine for thy stomach's sake and thine often infirmities." The waters of Asia Minor were alkaline and could interfere with the digestive system, which is what evidently happened to Timothy because he did have a stomach problem as well as other afflictions. Paul is advising Timothy to use this wine for medicinal purposes.[15]

> "Stomach wine," or "wine for the stomach," according to the writers of old Greek medicine, was a grape juice prepared as a thick, unfermented syrup for use as a food for dyspeptic and weak persons! Pliny, who lived in the apostolic age, wrote: "The beverage is given to invalids to whom it is apprehended that WINE may prove injurious." [Emphasis in the original.][16]

The Bible certainly doesn't condone drinking as some people would like to think. There are even many people professing to be Christians who drink (and, yes, even get drunk), but the Bible warns us that the drunkard will not enter heaven. Paul clearly writes:

> Now the works of the flesh are manifest, which are these: Adultery, fornication, uncleanness, lasciviousness, Idolatry, witchcraft, hatred, variance, emulations, wrath, strife, seditions, heresies, Envyings, murders, DRUNKENNESS, revellings, and such like: of the which I tell you before, as I have also told you in time past, that they which do such things SHALL NOT INHERIT the kingdom of God (Galatians 5:19-21).

Elsewhere Paul declares:

> Know ye not that the unrighteous SHALL NOT inherit the kingdom of God? Be not deceived: neither fornicators, nor idolaters, nor adulterers, nor effeminate, nor abusers of themselves with mankind, Nor thieves, nor covetous, nor DRUNKARDS, nor revilers, nor extortioners, shall inherit the kingdom of God (I Corinthians 6:9-10).

Are You Barred from Heaven?

Those who have committed the above sins (and "such like") are barred from heaven while they remain in their unforgiven state, but there is good news, for the very next verse says: "And such WERE some of you: BUT ye are washed, but ye are sanctified, but ye are justified in the name of the Lord Jesus, and by the Spirit of our God" (I Corinthians 6:11). AA literature tells us "'Once an alcoholic, always an alcoholic' is a simple fact we have to live with,"[17] but the Bible emphatically declares "such WERE some of you." "Were" is in the past, not the present, tense. There is hope for those who have committed sin, for "If we confess our sins, He [Jesus] is faithful and just to FORGIVE us our sins, and to CLEANSE us from all unrighteousness" (I John 1:9). Yes, alcoholism is a sin, but so are all the other items mentioned above. It doesn't matter if you are an adulterer, alcoholic, thief, covetous, etc., Christ is waiting with open arms to receive you unto Himself. Christ can take away the desire to sin (no matter what sin it is) and put a desire within you to live a righteous life. "If any man be in Christ, he is a new creature: OLD THINGS ARE PASSED AWAY; behold, all things are become new" (II Corinthians 5:17).

Perhaps you are reading this book and have never drunk any alcoholic beverages and you live a fairly decent life. Even though you may be a moral and honest person, if you have never invited Christ into your heart as your own PERSONAL Savior, you, too, are living in sin. Maybe you are not committing a blatant sin, but the Bible tells us that "ALL have sinned and come short of the glory of God" (Romans 3:23). The "ALL" includes both you and me, and "the wages of sin is [eternal] death; but the gift of God is eternal life through Jesus Christ our Lord" (Romans 6:23). God's gift to us is eternal life, but we must accept this gift to make the transaction valid. If I had a gift to give to you and you refused to accept it, that gift would do you no good. You must receive this gift for it to become effective.

Some Good News

Even though ALL of us are born in sin, the good news is that "Christ Jesus came into the world to save sinners" (I Timothy 1:15). If you have never accepted Christ as your PERSONAL Savior and would like to do so, the first step is to be born again. John 3:3:

"EXCEPT a man be born AGAIN, he CANNOT see the kingdom of God." How can one be born AGAIN? We all know that we were born once, our physical birth, but can we enter into our mother's womb and be born the second time (see John 3:1-17)? No. The second birth comes by being born into the family of God. John 3:16: "For God so LOVED the world [that includes YOU!] that He GAVE His only Begotten Son, that WHOSOEVER [that includes YOU] BELIEVETH [trusts, clings to, relies on] Him [God's Son, Jesus] should not perish [in hell], but have everlasting life." All you need to do is sincerely believe with all your heart that Jesus is the Son of God and to be willing to turn from your sins, whatever they are—big or small, and ask Jesus to come into your heart and help you to live for Him, and He WILL do it. "He that covereth his sins shall not prosper: but whoso CONFESSETH and FORSAKETH them shall have mercy" (Proverbs 28:13). John 6:37: "Him that cometh to Me I will IN NO WISE cast out." Romans 10:9: "If thou shalt CONFESS with thy mouth the Lord Jesus, and shalt BELIEVE in thine heart that God hath raised him from the dead, thou SHALT be saved [born again]."

If you would like to be born again, pray your own prayer or sincerely pray the following: *Dear Jesus, I realize that I am a sinner. I believe that You died for my sins. Please forgive me of my past sins and come into my heart. Save me for Your sake, and help me to live for You. I ask this in Your name. Amen.*

If you sincerely prayed and asked Jesus to forgive you of your sins, you will have the assurance that you are now a child of God. John 1:12: "But AS MANY as received Him, to them gave He power to become the sons of God, even to them that BELIEVE on His name." Read your Bible EVERY day (start with the book of John), and find a Bible-believing church where you can worship God with other born again believers.

The answer to overcoming an alcoholic lifestyle (or any other sin) is not found in attending Alcoholics Anonymous meetings, but in confessing your sins to Jesus and asking Him to forgive you. "For with the heart man believeth unto righteousness; and with the mouth confession is made unto salvation" (Romans 10:10). King David said: "I acknowledged my sin unto Thee [God], and mine iniquity have I not hid. I said, I will confess my transgressions unto the Lord; and Thou forgavest the iniquity of my sin" (Psalm 32:5).

"Therefore being justified by faith, we have peace with God through our Lord Jesus Christ" (Romans 5:1), "and the peace of God, which passeth all understanding, shall keep your hearts and minds through Christ Jesus" (Philippians 4:7). Isn't peace what the alcoholic is looking for in the first place? Attending AA meetings may bring companionship and a closeness with others who can sympathize with those who have gone through similar heartaches, but it can never meet the deepest yearnings in a person's life. AA can never impart peace to a troubled heart (especially while being involved with occultic practices) and it cannot bestow rest to a distressed and anguished soul. Only through Christ can these needs be met. Why settle for something superficial and temporary when genuine and lasting hope and peace is available through Christ?

Jesus knows the heartaches and burdens of the alcoholics. He has compassion on them and on every one else who is bearing the weight of sin. Gently He invites you: "Come unto Me, all ye that labour and are heavy laden, and I will give you rest" (Matthew 11:28).

> Have you ever been discouraged
>   And dissatisfied with life?
> Has your heart been filled with longings,
>   Wand'ring thru this world of strife?
> Come to Jesus—hear His pleading,
>   Come—there's rest and peace for thee;
> "Whosoever" is His promise,
>   Come—and thou shalt be made free.[18]

If the Son [Jesus Christ] therefore shall make you free, ye shall be free indeed" (John 8:36).

ENDNOTES:

CHAPTER 1: AA'S CO-FOUNDERS

1   "Alcoholism," *The World Book Illustrated Home Medical Encyclopedia* (1980), Vol. 1, p. 65.

2   *A Clergyman Asks about Alcoholics Anonymous* (New York, New York: Alcoholics Anonymous World Services, Inc., 1961), p. 4.

3   *The Co-Founders of Alcoholics Anonymous: Biographical Sketches* (New York, New York: Alcoholics Anonymous World Services, Inc., 1972), p. 18.

4   *Ibid.*, p. 6.

5   *Alcoholics Anonymous Comes of Age*, (New York: Harper & Brothers, 1957), pp. 58-59.

6   *Ibid.*, pp. 61-63.

7   *A Clergyman Asks about Alcoholics Anonymous, op. cit.*, p. 5.

8   *Alcoholics Anonymous Comes of Age, op. cit.*, pp. 65-66. See also *The Co-Founders of Alcoholics Anonymous: Biographical Sketches, op. cit.*, p. 6.; *A Clergyman Asks about Alcoholics Anonymous, op. cit.*, p. 4.

9   *Ibid.*, pp. 67-71. See also *The Co-Founders of Alcoholics Anonymous: Biographical Sketches, op. cit.*, pp. 6-7.; *A.A. Fact File* (New York, New York, 1956); *A Clergyman Asks about Alcoholics Anonymous, op. cit.*, p. 5.

10 *A Clergyman Asks about Alcoholics Anonymous, op. cit.*, p. 4.

11 *Alcoholics Anonymous Comes of Age, op. cit.*, p. 74.

12 *The Co-Founders of Alcoholics Anonymous: Biographical Sketches, op. cit.*, p. 7.

CHAPTER 2: WHO IS FRANK BUCHMAN

1   Tom Driberg, *The Mystery of Moral Re-Armament: A Study of Frank Buchman and His Movement* (New York: Alfred A. Knopf, Inc.), p. 11.

2   L. J. Trinterud, "Frank Buchman," *The World Book Encyclopedia,* 1961 edition, Vol. 2, p. 551. See also Driberg, *ibid.*

3   "Moral Rearmament," *Encyclopedia Britannica,* 1964 edition, Vol. 15, pp. 787-788.

4   Driberg, *op. cit.*, p. 52.

5   *Ibid.*

6   *Ibid.*, p. 12. See also Kenneth Scott Latourette, *A History of Christianity* (New York, New York: Harper & Row, 1953), p. 1419; L. J. Trinterud, "Frank Buchman," *The World Book Encyclopedia, op. cit.;* Texe Marrs, *Texe Marrs Book of New Age Cults & Religions* (Austin, Texas: Living Truth Publishers, 1990), p. 253; "Moral Re-Armament," *The World Book Encyclopedia,* 1961 edition, Vol. 12, p. 655.

7   Texe Marrs, *Texe Marrs Book of New Age Cults & Religions* (Austin, Texas: Living Truth Publishers, 1990), pp. 253-254. See also Texe Marrs, *Millennium: Peace, Promises, and the Day They Take Our Money Away* (Austin, Texas: Living Truth Publishers, 1990), pp. 248-249.

8   Driberg, *op. cit.* See also *Alcoholics Anonymous Comes of Age, op. cit.*, pp. 68, 75; Earle E. Cairns, *Christianity Through the Centuries: A History of the Christian Church* (Grand Rapid, Michigan: Zondervan Publishing House, 1954), p. 485; S. Stansfeld Sargent and Robert C. Williamson, *Social Psychology: An Introduction to the Study of Human Relations* (New York: The Ronald Press Company, 1958, 2nd edition), p. 528; "Moral Re-Armament" *The World Book Encyclopedia*, 1961 edition, Vol. 12, p. 655; "Moral Rearmament," *Encyclopedia Britannica, op. cit.*, p. 787.

9   Driberg, *ibid.*

10   *Ibid.*, p. 196.

11   Hensley Henson, quoted by Driberg, *ibid.*, pp. 197-198.

12   Texe Marrs, *Millennium: Peace, Promises, and the Day They Take Our Money Away* (Austin, Texas: Living Truth Publishers, 1990), p. 249.

13   Driberg, *op. cit.*, p. 194.

14   Texe Marrs, *Millennium, op. cit.*

15   Driberg, *op. cit.*

16   Texe Marrs, *Millennium, op. cit.*

17   *Ibid.*, p. 248.

18   Driberg, *op. cit.*, pp. 255-256.

19   S. Stansfeld Sargent and Robert C. Williamson, *Social Psychology: An Introduction to the Study of Human Relations* (New York: The Ronald Press Company, 1958, 2nd edition), p. 528. See also Texe Marrs, *Millennium, op. cit.*; Texe Marrs, *Texe Marrs Book of New Age Cults & Religions, op. cit.*, p. 253; Driberg, *op. cit.*, p. 64.

20   Texe Marrs, *Millennium, op. cit.*

21   Driberg, *op. cit.*, p. 67.

22   Frank Buchman, quoted by Driberg, *ibid.*, p. 65.

23   Texe Marrs, *Millennium, op. cit.*

24   Buchman, quoted by Driberg, *op. cit.*

25   *Ibid.*

26   *Ibid.*, p. 71.

27   *Ibid.*, p. 51.

28   *Ibid.*

CHAPTER 3: THE OXFORD GROUP'S LEGACY

1   *A.A. Fact File* (New York, New York: A.A. Publishing, Inc., 1956).

2   *Alcoholics Anonymous Comes of Age, op. cit.,* p. vii.

3   *Ibid.*

4   *Ibid.,* p. 165.

5   *Alcoholics Anonymous: The Story of How More Than One Hundred Men Have Recovered from Alcoholism* (New York, New York: Alcoholics Anonymous World Services, Inc., 1976, Third edition), p. 218.

6   *Alcoholics Anonymous Comes of Age, op. cit.,* pp. 74-75.

7   *Ibid.,* pp. 39-40.

8   *Ibid.,* p. 2.

9   *Ibid.,* pp. 39-40. See also pp. 253, 261.

10   Driberg, *op. cit.,* p. 267.

11   *Pass It On: The Story of Bill Wilson and How the AA Message Reached the World* (New York: Alcoholics Anonymous World Services, Inc. 1984), p. 280.

12   Lois Wilson, *Lois Remembers* (New York, New York: Al-Anon Family Groups Headquarters, Inc., 1979), p. 139.

CHAPTER 4: GOD—AS YOU UNDERSTAND HIM

1   *A Clergyman Asks about Alcoholics Anonymous, op. cit.,* p. 7. See also *Do You Think You're Different?* (New York, New York: Alcoholics Anonymous World Services, Inc., 1976), p. 30, etc.

2   Earle E. Cairns, *Christianity Through the Centuries: A History of the Christian Church* (Grand Rapids, Michigan: Zondervan Publishing House, 1954), p. 485.

3   S. Stansfeld Sargent and Robert C. Williamson, *op. cit.,* pp. 528-530.

4   *Twelve Steps and Twelve Traditions, op. cit.,* p. 112.

5   Wanda Marrs, *New Age Lies to Women* (Austin, Texas: Living Truth Publishers, 1989), pp. 178-179.

6   *A Clergyman Asks about Alcoholics Anonymous, op. cit.,* p. 11.

7   *44 Questions and Answers about the A.A. Program of Recovery from Alcoholism* (Works Publishing, Inc. [now known as Alcoholics Anonymous World Services, Inc.], 1952), p. 15.

8   *A Newcomer Asks...* (New York, New York: Alcoholics Anonymous World Services, Inc., 1981), p. 5.

9   *Alcoholics Anonymous* (New York, New York: Alcoholics Anonymous World Services, Inc., 1976, Third Edition), p. 248.

10   *Twelve Steps and Twelve Traditions, op. cit.,* pp.27-28, 110-111.

11 William Collins, "Spirituality: Watered-Down Religion, or Healing Tonic?" *The Harding Journal of Religion and Psychiatry* (Vol. 9. No. 2, 1990), pp. 7-8.

12 Martin and Deidre Bobgan, *Prophets of Psychoheresy II: Critiquing Dr. James C. Dobson* (Santa Barbara, California: EastGate Publishers, 1990), p. 250.

13 *Ibid.*, pp. 250-251.

14 *Ibid.*, p. 254.

15 Nan Robertson, *Getting Better: Inside Alcoholics Anonymous* (New York, New York: William Morrow and Company, Inc., 1988), p. 36.

16 *Ibid.*, pp. 36, 40, 84.

17 *Ibid.*, p. 85.

18 *Alcoholics Anonymous, op. cit.*, pp. 46-47.

19 Wanda Marrs, *New Age Lies to Women, op. cit.*, pp. 41-42.

20 *Ibid.*, pp. 45-46.

21 *Alcoholics Anonymous, op. cit.*, p. 503. See also *Alcoholics Anonymous Comes of Age, op. cit.*, p. 267.

22 *Alcoholics Anonymous Comes of Age, op. cit.*, p. 81.

CHAPTER 5: AA IS RELIGIOUS!

1 *A Clergyman Asks about Alcoholics Anonymous, op. cit.*, p. 15.

2 *Ibid.*, p. 11.

3 *Alcoholics Anonymous, op. cit.*, p. 47.

4 *Ibid.* p. 477.

5 *Alcoholics Anonymous Comes of Age, op. cit.*, p. 253.

6 *Alcoholics Anonymous, op. cit.*, p. 412.

7 *Ibid.*, p. 46.

8 *Ibid.*, p. 95.

9 *Alcoholics Anonymous Comes of Age, op. cit.*, p. 120.

10 *Ibid.*, p. 111.

11 *Ibid.*, p. 127.

12 *Ibid.*, p. 167.

13 *Ibid.*, p. 261.

14 *Alcoholics Anonymous, op. cit.*, p. 569.

15 *44 Questions and Answers about the A.A. Program of Recovery from Alcoholism, op. cit.*

16 *Twelve Steps and Twelve Traditions, op. cit.*, p. 112.

17 Wanda Marrs, *New Age Lies to Women, op. cit.,* p. 180.

18 Brochure from Coleman Publishing, n.p., n.d.

19 *Ibid.*

20 *What Can You Do about Someone Else's Drinking?,* (pamphlet distributed by the National Council on Alcoholism and Drug Dependence, Revised June 1990).

21 *Helping America Understand,* (brochure distributed by the National Council on Alcoholism and Drug Dependence, 1989 Annual Report), p. 2.

22 *Ibid.,* p. 4.

23 Robertson, *op. cit.,* p. 90.

24 *World Goodwill Newsletter* (1986, No. 2).

25 Brochure from World Service Forum, n.p., n.d.

26 *Alcoholics Anonymous Comes of Age, op. cit.,* p. 139.

27 *Ibid.*

28 Jerry Williams, "A Treatment Program That Fits the Need," *Addiction and Consciousness Journal* (Sept. 1988, Vol. 3, No. 3), p. 14.

29 *Ibid.*

30 Jon Klimo, "The Psychology of Channeling," *New Age Journal* (November/December 1987, Vol. 3, Issue 6), p. 36.

31 Douglas R. Groothuis, *Unmasking the New Age* (Downers Grove, Illinois: InterVarsity Press, 1986), pp. 47-48.

32 *Ibid.,* p. 47.

33 *Ibid.,* p. 48.

34 *Alcoholics Anonymous Comes of Age, op. cit.,* pp. 37, 253.

35 Fulton J. Sheen, "Jesuit," *The World Book Encyclopedia,* 1961 edition, Vol. 10, p. 81. See also Fulton J. Sheen, "St. Ignatius Loyola," *The World Book Encyclopedia,* 1961 edition, Vol. 11, pp. 443-444.

36 Edmond Paris, *The Secret History of the Jesuits* (Chino, California: Chick Publications, 1975), p. 21.

37 *Alcoholics Anonymous Comes of Age, op. cit.,* p. 167.

38 *Alcoholics Anonymous, op. cit.,* p. 55.

CHAPTER 6: AA'S GODPARENT: CARL JUNG

1 Catalog from CompCare Publishers, Spring 1991, p. 5.

2 "Carl Gustav Jung," *Encyclopedia Britannica,* 1964 edition, Vol. 13, p. 182.

3 Dave Hunt and T. A. McMahon, *America: The Sorcerer's New Apprentice: The Rise of New Age Shamanism* (Eugene, Oregon: Harvest House Publishers, 1988), p. 65.

4   "New Age Spirituality," *Llewellyn New Times*, #853, p. 47.

5   Colin Wilson, *The Occult: A History* (Random House, Inc., 1971), p. 249.

6   "Who's Who in Meditation," *Your Magical Self* (August 1985).

7   Harold G. Coward, "Psychology and Karma," *The American Theosophist*, (November 1983), p. 382.

8   Jung, quoted in *The Mysteries of Existence* (Wheaton, Illinois: The Theosophical Society in America, 1989, Revised printing), p. 17.

9   Caryl Matrisciana, "Gods of the New Age," *The Christian Reader* (July/August 1986), Vol. 24, No. 24., p. 100.

10   Nat Freedland, *The Occult Explosion* (New York: G. P. Putnam's & Sons, 1972), pp. 35-36.

11   Pat Means, *The Mystical Maze: A Guidebook Through the Mindfields of Eastern Mysticism* (Campus Crusade for Christ, Inc., 1976), p. 43.

12   Frank S. Leonard, "East As West: The I Ching As Holograph," *Chrysalis* (Autumn 1987, Vol. 2, Issue 3), p. 238.

13   Margot Adler, *Drawing Down the Moon: Witches, Druids, Goddess-Worshippers, and Other Pagans in America Today* (New York, New York: The Viking Press, 1979), p. 44. See also William J. Petersen, *Those Curious New Cults* (New Canaan, Connecticut: Keat Publishing, Inc.), p. 36.

14   Johanna Michaelsen, *Like Lambs to the Slaughter* (Eugene, Oregon: Harvest House Publishers, 1989), p. 37. See also Dave Hunt, *Beyond Seduction: A Return to Biblical Christianity* (Eugene, Oregon: Harvest House Publishers, 1987, p. 209.

15   For more information on Freemasonry and its occult connections, see my book entitled *Hidden Secrets of Masonry,* which can be obtain by writing to Sharing, 212 East Seventh Street (A), Mt. Carmel, PA 17851-2211.

16   Kathleen Klenetsky, "Charles, Prince of the New Age," *Executive Intelligence Review* (February 10, 1989, Vol. 16, No. 7), p. 32.

17   Hunt and McMahon, *America: The Sorcerer's New Apprentice, op. cit.,* p. 111.

18   Dave Hunt, *Beyond Seduction: A Return to Biblical Christianity* (Eugene, Oregon: Harvest House Publishers, 1987), p. 209.

19   Joseph Carr, *The Lucifer Connection* (Lafayette, Louisiana: Huntington House, Inc., 1987), p. 107.

20   Klenetsky, *op. cit.*

21   Stephen Larsen, "The Inner Guide," *Chrysalis* (Autumn 1987, Vol. 2, Issue 3), pp. 257-258.

22   Jung, quoted by Stephen Larsen in "The Inner Guide," *Chrysalis* (Autumn 1987, Vol. 2, Issue 3), p. 258.

23   Michaelsen, *op. cit.* See also Don Matzat, *Inner Healing: Deliverance or Deception?* (Eugene, Oregon: Harvest House Publishers, 1987), p. 84; Dave Hunt, *Beyond Seduction,*

op. cit., p. 210; Constance E. Cumbey, *A Planned Deception: The Staging of a New Age "Messiah"* (East Detroit, Michigan: Pointe Publishers, Inc., 1985), p. 21; Martin and Deidre Bobgan, *Psychoheresy: The Psychological Seduction of Christianity* (Santa Barbara, California: EastGate Publishers, 1987), p. 14; Klimo, "The Psychology of Channeling," *New Age Journal* (November/December 1987, Vol. 3, Issue 6), p. 62.

24   Stephen Larsen, "The Inner Guide," *Chrysalis, op. cit.,* p. 258.

25   Michaelsen, *op. cit.*

26   Carr, *op. cit.,* pp. 110-111. See also Klimo, "The Psychology of Channeling," *op. cit.*

27   Klimo, "The Psychology of Channeling," *ibid.*

28   Carr, *op. cit.,* p. 111.

29   Martin and Deidre Bobgan, *Psychoheresy: The Psychological Seduction of Christianity* (Santa Barbara, California: EastGate Publishers, 1987), p. 14.

30   Carl Jung, quoted by Colin Wilson in *The Occult: A History, op. cit.,* p. 478.

31   "Interesting Quotes," *CIB Bulletin* (August 1989), Vol. 5, No. 8, p. 4.

32   Freedland, *op. cit.,* p. 35.

33   *Ibid.,* p. 111.

34   More information on astrology can be acquired by writing for my article entitled "Astrology and Your Future."

35   Robert A. Morey, *Horoscopes and the Christian* (Minneapolis, Minnesota: Bethany House Publishers, 1981), p. 7. See also Kurt Koch, *Between Christ and Satan* (Grand Rapids, Michigan: Kregel Publications, 1972), p. 15.

36   *Alcoholics Anonymous, op. cit.,* pp. 26-27.

37   William Collins, "Spirituality: Watered-Down Religion, or Healing Tonic?" *The Harding Journal of Religion and Psychiatry, op. cit.,* p. 7.

38   Driberg, *op. cit.,* p. 194.

39   Texe Marrs, *Millennium, op. cit.*

40   Driberg, *op. cit.,* p. 12.

41   Texe Marrs, *Millennium, op. cit.*

42   "God Calling... or Devil on the Line?" *Flashpoint* (February 1991), p. 2. See also Texe Marrs, *Millennium, ibid.,* p. 252.

43   "Christian Bestsellers," *Virtue* (July/August 1990, Vol. 12, No. 6), p. 48. See also John Ankerberg and John Weldon, *The Facts on: The New Age Movement* (Chattanooga, Tennessee, 1988), p. 14; Wanda Marrs, *New Age Lies to Women, op. cit.,* p. 92.

44   *CIB Bulletin* (April 1990, Vol. 6, No. 4), p. 2.

45   Robertson, *op. cit.,* pp. 36, 84, 140. See also Texe Marrs, *Mystery Mark of the New Age: Satan's Design for World Domination,* (Westchester, Illinois: Crossway Books, 1988), p. 100.

46   Bobgan, *Psychoheresy, op. cit.*, pp. 12, 14.

47   *Alcoholics Anonymous, op. cit.*, pp. 11-12.

48   *Ibid.*, p. 12.

49   *Ibid.*

50   *Ibid.*

51   Albert James Dager, *Inner Healing: A Biblical Analysis* (Santa Ana, California: Tri-Level Press, 1986), p. 54.

52   Don Matzat, *Inner Healing: Deliverance or Deception?* (Eugene, Oregon: Harvest House Publishers, 1987), p. 69.

53   Dick Sutphen, "Ritual Magic," *Self-Help Update: Create Your Own Reality*, Issue 26, p. 12.

54   *Ibid.*

55   Charles Bensinger, *Chaco Journey: Remembrance and Awakening* (Sante Fe, New Mexico: Timewindow Publications, 1988), p. 193.

56   Brochure from Light of Christ Community Church.

57   Clifford Wilson and John Weldon, *Psychic Forces and Occult Shock: A Biblical View* (Chattanooga, Tennessee: Global Publishers, 1987), p. 54.

58   *Ibid.*

59   Eklal Kueshana, *The Ultimate Frontier* (Quinlan, Texas: The Stelle Group, 1986), pp. 97-98.

60   Shirley MacLaine, *Out on a Limb* (New York, New York: Bantam Books, Inc., 1983), p. 104.

61   *Ibid.*, p. 105.

62   Texe Marrs, *Texe Marrs Book of New Age Cults & Religions, op. cit.*, p. 254.

63   Texe Marrs, *Millennium, op. cit.*, p. 248.; See also Texe Marrs, *Texe Marrs Book of New Age Cults & Religions, op. cit.*, p. 253.

64   Means, *op. cit.*, p. 19.

65   Driberg, *op. cit.*, p. 163.

66   *Ibid.*, p. 167.

67   *Ibid.*, p. 177.

CHAPTER 7: IS ALCOHOLISM A DISEASE?

1   See Philip G. Zimbardo, *et. al.*, *Psychology and Life* (Glenview, Illinois: Scott, Foresman and Company, 1977); "Alcoholism," *Encyclopedia Britannica*, 1964 edition, Vol. 1, 1964; *A Clergyman Asks about Alcoholics Anonymous, op. cit.*; *This Is A.A.* (New York, New York: Alcoholics Anonymous Publishing, Inc. [now known as Alcoholics Anonymous

World Services, Inc.], 1984); *Do You Think You're Different?* (New York, New York: Alcoholics Anonymous World Services, Inc., 1976); *A Brief Guide to Alcoholics Anonymous* (New York, New York: Alcoholics Anonymous World Services, Inc., 1972); Wayne E. Oates, *The Christian Pastor* (Philadelphia, Pennsylvania: Westminster Press, 1964); *Let's Talk Facts about Substance Abuse* (Washington, D.C.: American Psychiatric Association, 1988); *Alcoholics Anonymous Comes of Age, op. cit.*; *Al-Anon Faces Alcoholism* (New York, New York: Al-Anon Family Groups Headquarters, Inc., 1981), etc.

2   "Alcoholism," *Encyclopedia Britannica*, Vol. 1, p. 547.

3   *This Is A.A.* (New York, New York: Alcoholics Anonymous, Inc., 1984), pp. 7, 10.

4   Rockwood, *Liquor: The Devil's "A" Bomb*, (Halifax, Canada: The People's Gospel Hour, n.d.) p. 7.

5   Bobgan, *Psychoheresy, op. cit.*, p. 139.

6   Harold Mulford, quoted in Bobgan, *Psychoheresy, ibid.*, pp. 139-140.

7   *What Can You Do about Someone Else's Drinking?, op. cit.*, p. 3.

8   *44 Questions and Answers about the A.A. Program of Recovery from Alcoholism. op. cit.*, p. 4.

9   *Do You Think You're Different?* (New York, New York: Alcoholics Anonymous World Services, Inc., 1976), p. 4.

10   Rockwood, *op. cit.*, pp. 7-8.

11   Taken from a tract entitled "Is Alcoholism a Disease?" See also Rockwood, *op. cit.*, p. 8.

12   Robertson, *op. cit.*, p. 256.

13   Dr. James C. Dobson, quoted in Bobgan, *Prophets of Psychoheresy II, op. cit.*, pp. 252-253.

14   Philip G. Zimbardo, *et. al.*, *Psychology and Life, op. cit.*, p. 468.

15   Mrs. Cyrus Osterhus, "We've Had a Barrel of Fun," *The Bible Friend* (October 1977, Vol. 74, No. 10), p. 2.

16   Bobgan, *Prophets of Psychoheresy II, op. cit.*, p. 252. See also Robertson, p. 91.

17   Robertson, *op. cit.*, p. 94.

18   Bobgan, *Prophets of Psychoheresy II, op. cit.*, pp. 251-252.

19   *Ibid.*, p. 252.

CHAPTER 8: "GAINS" AND LOSSES OF ALCOHOLISM

1   *Let's Talk Facts about Substance Abuse* (Washington, D.C.: American Psychiatric Association, 1988), p. 2.

2   *Christopher News Notes: Youth and Alcohol a Deadly Mix* (September 1990, No. 328), p. 3.

3   Raymond L. Cox, "The Great Deceiver" (Tract published by Pilgrim Tract Society, Inc.), p. 1.

4   *Christopher News Notes, op. cit.*

5   David C. Egner, "An Age-Old Problem," *Our Daily Bread* (May 1991), Vol. 36, No. 2.

6   *Ibid.*, p. 2.

7   "Youth and Alcohol" (a fact sheet from the National Council on Alcoholism and Drug Dependence).

8   *Ibid.*

9   *Ibid.*

10 "Alcoholism and Alcohol-Related Problems" (a fact sheet from the National Council on Alcoholism and Drug Dependence).

11 *Let's Talk Facts about Teen Suicide* (Washington, D.C.: American Psychiatric Association, 1988), p. 3.

12 "Youth and Alcohol," *op. cit.*

13 Walter Wink, "Biting the Bullet: The Case for Legalizing Drugs," *The Christian Century* (August 8-15, 1990, Vol. 107, No. 23). p. 738.

14 *Ibid.*

15 *Ibid.* See also "Alcoholism and Alcohol-Related Problems," *op. cit.*

16 Egner, *op. cit.*

17 *Let's Talk Facts about Substance Abuse, op. cit.*, p. 1.

18 "Alcoholism and Alcohol-Related Problems," *op. cit.*

19 *Ibid.*

20 *Ibid.*

21 Egner, *op. cit.*

22 Mrs. Cyrus Osterhus, "News Bits from Here and There," *The Bible Friend* (October 1977, Vol. 74, No. 10), p. 9.

23 Rockwood, *op. cit.*, p. 10.

24 Cyrus Osterhus, "Liquor Is an Enemy of Body and Soul" (Tract published by Osterhus Publishing), p. 3.

25 "Prohibition" (flyer distributed by Signal Press).

26 *A Brief Guide to Alcoholics Anonymous* (New York, New York: Alcoholics Anonymous World Services, Inc., 1972), p. 2.

27 *Let's Talk Facts about Substance Abuse, op. cit.*, pp. 3-4.

28 "Alcoholism," *Encyclopedia Britannica* 1964 edition, Vol. 1, p. 550. See also *Let's Talk Facts about Substance Abuse, ibid.*

29 "The Bar" (a Tract published by Old Paths Tract Society).

30 Cox, *op. cit.*

31 "Protect Your Home!!" (Tract published by Pilgrim Tract Society, n.d.).

32   "If," *Dynamic Preaching* (June 1989, Vol. 4; No. 6), pp. 15-16.

CHAPTER 9: ADULT CHILDREN OF ALCOHOLICS

1   *Al-Anon Faces Alcoholism* (New York, New York: Al-Anon Family Groups Headquarters, Inc., 1981), p. 286.

2   *Ibid.*, no page number listed.

3   Robertson, *op. cit.*, p. 176.

4   *Ibid.*, p. 178.

5   For a more thorough explanation of these occult subjects, request my articles entitled "What Is Visualization?" and "A Look at Inner Healing."

6   Rita Prince Winston, "Trance, Relaxation and Adventure," *Circle Network News*, Vol. 10, No. 1 (Spring 1988), p. 11.

7   Emrika Padus, *et. al.*, *The Complete Guide to Your Emotions and Your Health* (Emmaus, Pennsylvania: Rodale Press, 1986), p. 266.

8   Llewellyn's New Worlds' advertisement for a book by Melita Denning and Osborne Phillips entitled *Creative Visualization*, p. 11.

9   *Llewellyn New Times*, (July/August, #864), p. 45.

10   *Spirit Speaks: Life in the Spirit World*, Issue 7, pp. 28-29.

11   Matzat, *op. cit.*, p. 80.

12   "Does Jesus Care?", song written by Frank E. Graeff.

13   "He Knows Just What I Need," song written by Mosie Lister, 1955.

CHAPTER 10: THE BIBLE AND ALCOHOLISM

1   *A Clergyman Asks about Alcoholics Anonymous, op. cit.*, p. 4.

2   *Ibid.*, pp. 7-8.

3   *44 Questions and Answers about the A.A. Program of Recovery from Alcoholism, op. cit.*, p. 16.

4   *Alcoholics Anonymous, op. cit.*, pp. 100-103.

5   *Ibid.*

6   Robert V. Seliger, *It's Smarter Not to Drink: A Brief Medical Discussion* (Columbus, Ohio: School and College Service, 1953), p. 15.

7   *Ibid.*, pp. 7, 27.

8   Jeffrey R. M. Kunz and Asher J. Finkel, eds., *The American Medical Association Family Medical Guide*, (New York: Random House, 1987), p. 35.

9   *Ibid.*, p. 37.

10   Donald W. Hewitt, "Death in the Bottle: The Confessions of a Moderate Drinker," (Tract published by Old Paths Tract Society, Inc., n.d.), p. 2.

11   *Ibid.,* p. 6.

12   Stan Schirmacher, "Wine! It's in the Bible" (Tract published by Osterhus Publishing House, n.d.).

13   *Ibid.*

14   Rockwood, *op. cit.,* pp. 6-7.

15   *Ibid.,* p. 5.

16   Schirmacher, *op. cit.*

17   *This is A.A., op. cit.,* p. 7.

18   "Come to Jesus," song written by Albert H. Heinz, 1967.

BIBLIOGRAPHY

44 Questions and Answers about the A.A. Program of Recovery from Alcoholism (New York, New York: Works Publishing, Inc. [now known as Alcoholics Anonymous World Services, Inc.], 1952).

A Brief Guide to Alcoholics Anonymous (New York, New York: Alcoholics Anonymous World Services, Inc., 1972).

A Clergyman Asks about Alcoholics Anonymous (New York, New York: Alcoholics Anonymous World Services, Inc., 1961).

"A Drunkard's Reward for Drinking Alcohol" (Tract published by Osterhus Publishing House, n.d.).

A.A. at a Glance (New York, New York: Alcoholics Anonymous World Services, Inc., 1989).

A.A. Fact File (New York, New York: A.A. Publishing, Inc. [now known as Alcoholics Anonymous World Services, Inc.], 1956).

A.A. Member, The (New York, New York: Alcoholics Anonymous World Services, Inc., 1984).

AA Membership Survey (New York, New York: Alcoholics Anonymous World Services, Inc., 1989 Reprint).

ACA Program and How It Works, The (Torrance, California: Adult Children of Alcoholics, November 10, 1984).

Al-Anon Faces Alcoholism (New York, New York: Al-Anon Family Groups Headquarters, Inc., 1981).

Alcohol: Who Is Allergic? (Culver City, California: Eversharp, Inc., 1966).

Alcoholics Anonymous (New York, New York: Alcoholics World Services, Inc., 1976, Third Edition).

Alcoholics Anonymous: The Story of How More Than One Hundred Men Have Recovered from Alcoholism (New York City, New York: Works Publishing Company, 1939).

Alcoholics Anonymous Comes of Age (New York: Harper & Brothers, 1957).

Alcoholics Anonymous in Your Community (New York, New York: Alcoholics Anonymous World Services, Inc., 1990 Reprint).

"Alcoholism," *Encyclopedia Britannica,* Vol. 1, 1964 Edition.

"Alcoholism," *The World Book Illustrated Home Medical Encyclopedia* (1980), Vol. 1, p. 65.

"Alcoholism and Alcohol-Related Problems" (fact sheet from National Council on Alcoholism and Drug Dependence).

"Alcoholism, Other Drug Addictions and Related Problems among Women" (fact sheet from National Council on Alcoholism and Drug Dependence).

Alder, Margot. *Drawing Down the Moon: Witches, Druids, Goddess-Worshippers, and Other Pagans in America Today* (New York, New York: The Viking Press, 1979).

Alexander, Brooks. "A Generation of Wizards: Shamanism and Contemporary Culture Part II," *SCP Newsletter,* March/April 1983.

Ankerberg, John, and John Weldon. *The Facts On: The New Age Movement* (Chattanooga, Tennessee: The John Ankerberg Evangelistic Association, 1988).

"AP Trends," *AP Leader,* Winter 1991, Vol. 7, No. 1.

Atlanta Metaphysician, Volume 1, Issue 11.

"Beer Belongs" (Tract published by Pilgrim Tract Society, Inc., n.d.).

Bensinger, Charles. *Chaco Journey: Remembrance and Awakening* (Sante Fe, New Mexico: Timewindow Publications, 1988).

Bobgan, Martin and Deidre. *Prophets of Psychoheresy II: Critiquing Dr. James C. Dobson* (Santa Barbara, California: EastGate Publishers, 1990).

Bobgan, Martin and Deidre. *Psychoheresy: The Psychological Seduction of Christianity* (Santa Barbara, California: EastGate Publishers, 1987).

Boyd, James P. *Bible Dictionary* (New York: Ottenheimer Publishers, Inc., 1958).

Cairns, Earle E. *Christianity Through the Centuries: A History of the Christian Church* (Grand Rapids, Michigan: Zondervan Publishing House, 1954).

"Carl Gustav Jung," *Encyclopedia Britannica,* Vol. 13, 1964 edition.

Carr, Joseph. *The Lucifer Connection* (Lafayette, Louisiana: Huntington House, Inc., 1987).

"Christian Bestsellers," *Virtue,* July/August 1990.

Christopher News Notes: Youth and Alcohol a Deadly Mix, September, 1990.

CIB Bulletin, April 1990.

Clark, Kenneth E. "Carl Gustav Jung," *The World Book Encyclopedia,* Vol. 10, 1961 edition.

Clinebell, Howard J., Jr. *Basic Types of Pastoral Counseling* (Tennessee: Abingdon Press, 1966).

Co-Founders of Alcoholics Anonymous: Biographical Sketches, The (New York, New York: Alcoholics Anonymous World Services, Inc., 1972).

Collins, Gary R. *Can You Trust Psychology? Exposing the Facts and the Fictions* (Downers Grove, Illinois: InterVarsity Press, 1988).

Collins, William. "Spirituality: Watered-Down Religion or Healing Tonic?" *The Harding Journal of Religion and Psychiatry,* 1990.

Coward, Harold G. "Psychology and Karma," *The American Theosophist,* November 1983.

Cox, Raymond L. "The Great Deceiver" (Tract published by Pilgrim Tract Society, Inc., n.d.).

Cumbey, Constance E.: *A Planned Deception: The Staging of a New Age "Messiah"* (East Detroit, Michigan: Pointe Publishers, Inc., 1985).

Dager, Albert James. *Inner Healing: A Biblical Analysis* (Santa Ana, California: Tri-Level Press, 1986).

Dahlberg, Swan A. "We've Had a Barrel of Fun," *The Bible Friend,* October 1977.

"Directory of New Age Resources," *New Age Journal,* November/December 1988.

Do You Think You're Different? (New York, New York: Alcoholics Anonymous World Services, Inc., 1976).

Driberg, Tom. *The Mystery of Moral Re-Armament: A Study of Frank Buchman and His Movement* (New York: Alfred A. Knopf, Inc., 1965).

Egner, David C. "An Age-Old Problem," *Our Daily Bread* (May 1991), Vol. 36, No. 2.

English, O. Spurgeon, and Gerald H. J. Pearson. *Emotional Problems of Living: Avoiding the Neurotic Pattern* (New York: W. W. Norton and Company, Inc., 1963, Third Edition.

Epperson, A. Ralph. *The Unseen Hand: An Introduction to the Conspiratorial View of History* (Tucson, Arizona: Publius Press, 1985).

Finding Wholeness Through Separation: The Paradox of Independence (Torrance, California: Adult Children of Alcoholics, January 19, 1986).

Flora, Emmitt W. "Drunken Drivers" (Tract published by Old Paths Tract Society, n.d.).

Freedland, Nat. *The Occult Explosion* (New York: G. P. Putnam's & Sons, 1972).

Gauld, Alan. *The Founders of Psychical Research* (New York, New York: Shocken Books, Inc., 1968).

Godwin, John. *Occult America* (Garden City, New Jersey: Doubleday and Company, Inc., 1972.

"God Calling... or Devil on the Line?", *Flashpoint,* February 1991.

Griffith, Des. *Fourth Reich of the Rich* (Emissary Publications, 1978).

Groothuis, Douglas R. *Unmasking the New Age* (Downers Grove, Illinois: InterVarsity Press, 1986).

Hewitt, Donald W. "Death in the Bottle: The Confessions of a Moderate Drinker" (Tract published by Old Paths Tract Society, Inc., n.d.).

How AA Members Cooperate with Other Community Efforts to Help Alcoholics (New York, New York: Alcoholics Anonymous World Services, Inc., 1990 Reprint).

Hunt, Dave. *Beyond Seduction: A Return to Biblical Christianity* (Eugene, Oregon: Harvest House Publishers, 1987).

Hunt, Dave, and T. A. McMahon. *America: The Sorcerer's New Apprentice: The Rise of New Age Shamanism* (Eugene, Oregon: Harvest House Publishers, 1988).

Hunt, Dave, and T. A. McMahon. *The Seduction of Christianity: Spiritual Discernment in the Last Days* (Eugene, Oregon: Harvest House Publishers, 1985).

Hunter, Sidney. *Is Alberto for Real?* Chino, California: Chick Publications, 1988).

"If," *Dynamic Preaching,* June 1989.

Importance of Service in ACA, The (Torrance, California: Adult Children of Alcoholics, January 17, 1987).

"Interesting Quotes," *CIB Bulletin,* August 1989.

"Is Alcoholism a Disease?" (Tract published Old Paths Tract Society, Inc., n.d.).

"Key in Whiskey, The." (Tract published by Old Paths Tract Society, Inc., n.d.).

Klenetsky, Kathleen. "Charles, Prince of the New Age," *Executive Intelligence Review,* February 10, 1989.

Klimo, Jon. "The Psychology of Channeling," *New Age Journal,* November/December 1987.

Koch Kurt. *Between Christ and Satan* (Grand Rapids, Michigan: Kregel Publications, 1972).

Koch, Kurt. *Occult ABC* (Germany: Literature Mission Aglasterhausten, Inc., 1978).

Kueshana, Eklal. *The Ultimate Frontier* (Quinlan, Texas: The Stelle Group, 1986).

Kunz, Jeffrey R. M., and Asher H. Finkel, eds. *The American Medical Association Family Medical Guide* (New York: Random House, 1987).

Latourette, Kenneth Scott. *A History of Christianity* (New York, New York: Harper & Row, 1953).

Leonard, Frank S. "East As West: The I Ching As Holograph," *Chrysalis,* Autumn 1987.

Let's Talk Facts about Substance Abuse (Washington, D.C.: American Psychiatric Association, 1988).

Let's Talk Facts about Teen Suicide (Washington, D.C.: American Psychiatric Association, 1988).

Llewellyn's New Worlds (catalog).

MacLaine, Shirley. *Out on a Limb* (New York, New York: Bantam Books, Inc., 1983).

Marrs, Texe. *Millennium: Peace, Promises, and the Day They Take Our Money Away* (Austin, Texas: Living Truth Publishers, 1990).

Marrs, Texe. *Mystery Mark of the New Age: Satan's Design for World Domination* (Westchester, Illinois: Crossway Books, 1988).

Marrs, Texe. *Texe Marrs Book of New Age Cults & Religious* (Austin, Texas: Living Truth Publishers, 1990).

Marrs, Wanda. *New Age Lies to Women* (Austin, Texas: Living Truth Publishers, 1989).

Matrisciana, Caryl. "Gods of the New Age," *The Christian Reader,* July/August 1986.

Matzat, Don. *Inner Healing: Deliverance or Deception?* (Eugene, Oregon: Harvest House Publishers, 1987).

McMillen, S. I. *None of These Diseases* (Old Tappan, New Jersey: Fleming H. Revell Company, 1974).

Means, Pat. *The Mystical Maze: A Guidepost Through the Mindfields of Eastern Mysticism* (Campus Crusade for Christ, Inc., 1976).

Michaelsen, Johanna. *Like Lambs to the Slaughter* (Eugene, Oregon: Harvest House Publishers, 1989).

"Moral Re-Armament," *The World Book Encyclopedia,* Vol. 12, 1961 edition.

"Moral Rearmament," *Encyclopedia Britannica,* Vol. 15, 1964 edition.

Morey, Robert. A. *Horoscopes and the Christian* (Minneapolis, Minnesota: Bethany House Publishers, 1981).

Mysteries of Existence (Wheaton, Illinois: The Theosophical Society in America, 1989, Second Printing).

"National Council on Alcoholism and Drug Dependence 1989 Annual Report" (report from National Council on Alcoholism and Drug Dependence).

"New Age Spirituality," *Llewellyn New Times* #853.

Oates, Wayne E. *The Christian Pastor* (Philadelphia, Pennsylvania: Westminster Press, 1964).

Osbeck, Kenneth W. *101 More Hymn Stories* (Grand Rapids, Michigan: Kregel Publications, 1985).

Osterhus, Cyrus. "Liquor Is an Enemy of Body and Soul" (Tract published by Osterhus Publishing, n.d.).

Osterhus, Cyrus. "Old Alcohol Will Have to Fall" (Tract published by Osterhus Publishing Company, n.d.).

Padus, Emrika, *et. al. The Complete Guide to Your Emotions and Your Health* (Emmaus, Pennsylvania: Rodale Press, 1986).

Paris, Edmond. *The Secret History of the Jesuits* (Chino, California: Chick Publications, 1975).

Petersen, William J. *Those Curious New Cults* (New Canaan, Connecticut: Keat Publishing, Inc., 1975).

"Protect Your Home!!" (Tract published by Pilgrim Tract Society, n.d.).

Quick, Daryl E. *The Healing Journey for Adult Children of Alcoholics* (Downers Grove, Illinois: InterVarsity Press, 1990).

Reese, W. L. *Dictionary of Philosophy and Religion: Eastern and Western Thought* (Atlantic Highlands, New Jersey: Humanities Press, Inc., 1980).

Robertson, Nan. *Getting Better: Inside Alcoholics Anonymous* (New York, New York: William Morrow and Company, Inc., 1988).

Rockwood, Perry F. *Liquor: The Devil's "A" Bomb* (Halifax, Canada: The Peoples Gospel Hour).

Runes, Dagobert D. *Treasury of Philosophy* (New York, New York: Philosophical Library, 1955).

Sargent, S. Stansfeld, and Robert C. Williamson. *Social Psychology: An Introduction to the Study of Human Relations* (New York: The Ronald Press Company, 1958, Second Edition).

Schirmacher, Stan. "Wine! It's in the Bible" (Tract published by Osterhus Publishing House, n.d.).

Seamens, Dan. "Compass: News from the Universe," *East West: The Journal of Natural Health and Living,* February 1989.

Self-Help Update: Create Your Own Reality, Issue 26.

Seliger, Robert V. *It's Smarter Not to Drink: A Brief Medical Discussion* (Columbus, Ohio:

School and College Service, 1953).

Sheen, Fulton J. "Jesuit," *The World Book Encyclopedia,* 1961), Vol. 10.

Sheen, Fulton J. "Saint Ignatius Loyola," *The World Book Encyclopedia,* 1961), Vol. 11.

Shelhamer, Mrs. E. E. "A Bottle of Liquor" (Tract published by Pilgrim Tract Society, Inc., n.d.).

Spirit Speaks: Life in the Spirit World, Issue 7.

Strong, James. *Strong's Exhaustive Concordance of the Bible* (Lynchburg, Virginia: The Old-Time Gospel Hour, n.d.).

This Is A.A. (New York, New York: Alcoholics Anonymous Publishing, Inc. [now known as Alcoholics Anonymous World Services, Inc.], 1984.

Thomsen, Russel J. *Medical Wisdom from the Bible* (Old Tappan, New Jersey: Fleming H. Revell Company, 1974).

Trinterud, L. J. "Frank Buchman," *The World Book Encyclopedia,* Vol. 2, 1961 edition.

Twelve Steps and Twelve Traditions (New York: Harper & Brothers, 1952).

Vine, W. E. *Vine's Expository Dictionary of New Testament Words* (Lynchburg, Virginia: The Old-Time Gospel Hour, n.d.).

Welcome Newcomer (Torrance, California: Adult Children of Alcoholics).

"What Are the Signs of Alcoholism?" (fact sheet from National Council on Alcoholism and Drug Dependence).

"What Can You Do About Someone Else's Drinking?" (pamphlet from the National Council on Alcoholism and Drug Dependence).

"Who's Who in Meditation," *Your Magical Self,* August 1985.

Williams, Jerry. "A Treatment Program That Fits the Need," *Addiction and Consciousness Journal,* September 1988.

Wilson, Clifford, and John Weldon. *Psychic Forces and Occult Shock: A Biblical View* (Chattanooga, Tennessee: Global Publishers, 1987).

Wilson, Colin. *The Occult: A History* (Random House, Inc., 1971).

Wink, Walter. "Biting the Bullet: The Case for Legalizing Drugs," *The Christian Century,* August 8-15, 1990.

Winston, Rita Prince. "Trance, Relaxation and Adventure," *Circle Network News,* Spring 1988.

World Goodwill Newsletter, 1986, #2.

World Service Forum, (n.p., n.d.).

Wuest, Kenneth S. *Wuest's Word Studies from the Greek New Testament,* Vol. 3 (Grand Rapids, Michigan: William B. Eerdmans Publishing Company, 1973).

"Youth and Alcohol" (fact sheet from the National Council on Alcoholism and Drug Dependence).

Zimbardo, Philip G., *et. al. Psychology and Life* (Glenview, Illinois: Scott, Foresman and Company, 1977).

OTHER LITERATURE
BY CATHY BURNS

BOOKS:

Alcoholics Anonymous Unmasked (126 pages) $5.95

Hidden Secrets of Masonry (64 pages) .... $ 3.95

Hidden Secrets of the Eastern Star $12.95

BOOKLETS: .... **$0.50 each**

Astrology and Your Future

Eternal Life

Hypnosis: Cure or Curse?

Questions and Answers About the New Age Movement

To Catholics with Love

What Is Your I.Q.?

ARTICLES: .... **$0.50 each**
(except where noted)

Chart Your Course with Orion International

Divination

Divorce and Remarriage

Dowsing Is in the Bible!

Hidden Dangers of Reflexology

I Have Sinned

Jason Winters and His Herbal Tea

Miscegenation

Mormonism (3 part series) $1.50

1. Mormonism and Its History

2. Some Doctrines of Mormonism

3. Mormonism and Godhood

New Age Love

Some Occult Terms Explained

The Rapture—When Will It Occur?

Tongues and Related Issues (14 part series) $5.00
1. Do All Speak in Tongues?

2. Baptism in the Holy Ghost

3. Sinful Lives and Tongues

4. Signs and Wonders

5. Prosperity and Riches

6. The Power of Words

7. Can We Create Our Own Reality?

8. What Is Visualization?

9. A Look at Inner Healing

10. Are You a God?

11. Misfits Removed!

12. Renegades Excluded!

13. Thy Kingdom Come!

14. Will the Church Be Raptured?

Unity or D-i-v-i-s-i-o-n?

Witchcraft in the Church